A FARTHER SHORE

Ruth Patterson

Published 2000 by
Veritas Publications
7/8 Lower Abbey Street
Dublin 1

ISBN 1 85390 545 3

British Library Cataloguing
in Publication Data.
A catalogue record for
this book is available
from the British Library.

Cover design by Barbara Croatto
Printed in the Republic of Ireland by Betaprint Ltd, Dublin

History says, Don't hope
On this side of the grave,
But then, once in a lifetime
The longed-for tidal wave
Of justice can rise up,
And hope and history rhyme

So hope for a great sea-change
On the far side of revenge.
Believe that a farther shore
Is reachable from here.

– Seamus Heaney, 'The Cure At Troy'
(*Opened Ground Poems 1966-1996*
[London: Faber & Faber Ltd, 1998], p. 330).

CONTENTS

Acknowledgements

My grateful thanks go to members of my family and to the many friends of Restoration Ministries who helped and supported me in bringing this book to fruition. A special thank-you to Jean Vanier for writing the foreword, to Eithne Agnew for all the work behind the scenes, not least in typing the manuscript, and to Veritas for their advice, encouragement and assistance at every stage.

FOREWORD

I love Ireland. Is it because my grandmother was a Maloney from County Clare? Or is it because of the Irish people's friendliness, their faith, their laughter, their jokes, or because of the windy, rainy days and the land frequently surrounded by angry waves?

One day, however, I discovered another Ireland – huge wire barriers separating streets in Belfast, guns held sometimes by young, fearful soldiers from England, mothers telling me of their sons killed by 'the other side', their bodies left lying in the open streets, people in the South asking 'Aren't you afraid to go up there?' – two faces of Ireland reflecting two sides in each one of us: the place of faith and laughter and the more hidden place of fear and darkness.

Then I met the Corrymeela community: a sign of hope, where both 'sides' come together and are welcomed in love. They begin to meet each other. Person to person. Heart to heart. No one is seen any longer as being part of 'the other side' but simply as a person, a heart, a wounded heart. Barriers begin to fall. A communion of hearts is born. Life begins to flow. Hope rises up.

In 1975 I met Ruth Patterson when a group of people from different Christian traditions came together to organise an ecumenical 'Festival of Faith and Friendship', which took place the following June. There, some 150 people came together to pray and worship and sing, to listen to the words of Jesus, to meet each other and celebrate. We reflected together on the Beatitudes, on violence, on conflict resolution, on forgiveness and on peacemaking. We ended by washing each other's feet as Jesus asked us to do. A ceasefire had been declared just a few months earlier, so the perfume of peace quietly filled the air.

While in Belfast I visited Restoration Ministries. I saw and heard the passion for peace that filled the heart and work of Reverend Ruth Patterson, the first woman ordained as a minister in the Presbyterian Church in Ireland. I witnessed her passionate love for Jesus and her yearnings for His Kingdom of peace to come, her desire for truth, her capacity to take risks and to walk on untreaded and uncharted land.

This book tells of her journey as a living, faithful friend and disciple of Jesus. It is a book filled with a song of hope, a hope in God flowing out of a pain-filled land, a divided people, where the smell of death and civil war is present too; where people of different Christian traditions can sometimes strongly and fearfully hide behind the barriers of their certitudes and their refusal to meet those from 'the other side'.

I believe that Northern Ireland has a message for the rest of the world. Does not the light of hope in Jesus shine out more clearly and strongly in places of darkness, where human hope is failing? In the North many men and women are risking their lives for peace, followers of Jesus who take His message seriously. This message is chartered in the Beatitudes, in the love of enemies, in forgiveness, in Jesus' presence in the poor and the downtrodden, in His gift of the Holy Spirit. Ruth Patterson is one of these followers of Jesus.

It is important to listen to her and to others who, in the midst of darkness and despair, see the light of dawn emerging. Christians all over the world are being called today to discover that, in and with Jesus, a new hope is given, that with Him, the impossible can become possible. We are all called to the risk and folly of belief in Jesus.

Jean Vanier

INTRODUCTION

I have never written a book before. It has been an awesome and an exciting experience. The second part came into being first, over a longer period of time; originally, I thought it would be an entity in itself, but not so. The reflective poems that comprise the second half of the book were, I believe, 'given' at certain stages of the journey – particular times that were an integral part of my own travelling. They also speak in some little way of the journey of Ireland over the last turbulent years of our history. The first part of the book came later, and had to be completed within a given timespan. Today I have written the last sentence, and now I return to the beginning. Outside there is a rare burst of sunshine in the otherwise grey and leaden skies, which seem to have become part of Irish summers in the last few years. Arthur, one of our faithful volunteers at Restoration House, is working in the garden. For a brief spell, all is quietness, broken only by the sound of the Dublin train thundering reassuringly past on the line that borders our front garden. I look back over the past few weeks and, as well as breathing a prayer of gratitude, also heave a sigh of relief. There were times when I thought I'd never make it! What was scheduled to be an uninterrupted spell for writing has been punctuated with all sorts of comings and goings, both of great and of little import.

While we have had the most peaceful 'marching season' for several years, the future of the Northern Ireland Peace Process is hanging in the balance. The whole community has been living at the edge during these weeks, with hope and despair, expectancy and disappointment going hand in hand. Although activities at Restoration House tend to wind down over the summer in order that the volunteers themselves may be restored, much has still been happening. There have been

several weary pilgrims seeking rest and someone to 'hear' them.
About fifty young French people, on a journey of reconciliation, have
stopped off here to listen and to ask questions. Some crisis calls of
distress have been followed by the joy of seeing smiles after tears, like
sunshine after rain. I have had the rare honour of being invited, as a
Presbyterian, to give the homily at a Silver Jubilee Mass for a dear
friend from the Society of African Missions, and the privilege of
attending an evening at Áras an Uachtaráin to celebrate an island of
cultural diversity and to commemorate Douglas Hyde, the first
President of Ireland, who happened to be a Protestant. In the midst
of all of this, a new surface was being put on our carpark, creating
great upheaval for one precious day, including ornaments crashing off
the mantelpiece as the machinery vibrated outside. But the end result
has been worth it. And in the personal, very mundane world of Ruth,
I have had repeated visits to the dentist, as one tooth after another
seemed to go into rebellion and require complicated treatment. This,
and much more, is the stuff of which all our lives are made – the
ordinary and the extraordinary.

Through it all, I have sought to recall and reflect on my journey,
and on some of the events and experiences that have stretched and
moulded and shaped me into who I am today. There are many times
when I feel that I am still only at the starting point, that I am still an
inexperienced and stumbling pilgrim. What is up ahead is as yet
unknown, but of this I am very certain: God has something in mind
for all who seek to journey, something that is far beyond what we
could ever hope for, or even imagine. I believe that, for myself, for
you who read, for Ireland, for the Church and for the world, a
farther shore is reachable from here. While what I have shared is on
one level very personal, I trust that you may find some
encouragement for your journey also, and that you, too, will know
that the best is yet to be.

July 1999

PART ONE

STAGES ON MY JOURNEY

CHAPTER ONE

SETTING OUT

'There's no sense in going further – it's the edge of cultivation.'
So they said, and I believed it – broke my land and sowed my crop –
...Till a voice as bad as Conscience, rang interminable changes
On one everlasting Whisper day and night repeated – so:
'Something hidden. Go and find it. Go and look behind the Ranges –
Something lost behind the Ranges. Lost and waiting for you. Go!'
Yes, your 'Never, never country' – yes, your 'edge of cultivation'
And 'no sense in going further' – till I crossed the range to see.
God forgive me! No, I didn't. It's God's present to our nation.
Anybody might have found it, but – His Whisper came to me!

         – Rudyard Kipling, 'The Explorer'[1]

I never remember a time when I was not aware of 'something more'. There has always been that sense within me of more to be discovered or revealed. So the concept of life as a journey, of faith as a journey, has been one through which I find it helpful to express myself. From somewhere, even at times of weariness or discouragement, there has come the whisper of 'up ahead' that brings me to my feet again, ready to keep on travelling for the sake of that something more. Paradoxically, there is also the urge or the temptation to settle, to see a certain stage as a permanent resting place, where I plough my land and sow my crops. This is often the louder voice, because it comes not only from many well-meaning, good people concerned for my

---

1. Rudyard Kipling, *The Definitive Edition of Rudyard Kipling's Verse* (London: Hodder and Stoughton Ltd, 1994), pp. 103-4, 107.

welfare, but also from deep within the shadows of my own being where lurk inadequacies, doubts and fears. It is so easy to believe them, to accept the fact that there's no sense in going further, that here is the edge of cultivation. It has to be said that sometimes both inner and outer voices are right, and I have been, and am, eternally grateful to them. At other points, however, they need to be resisted in such a way that it is possible for me to hear the everlasting whisper and believe that there is something hidden behind the ranges, lost and waiting, and that I have to go, to move on. What is up ahead does not belong to me. It is always God's gift, waiting to be discovered, and its purpose is to bless the world. For those who dare to listen, who hear, who set out, the gift can be a costly, two-edged one. While anyone can find it, there is a sense that it is tailor-made for each individual to discover. What we hope for in life can remain a 'never, never country', or it can assume reality. There is a difference between dream and vision, between wishful thinking and a goal that beckons. We are grasped by vision; we are urged forward towards a goal. If His whisper comes to me, then I cannot ignore it.

One of the people who inspires me most when I think of such a journey is Abraham. He was willing, at the age of seventy-five, to say goodbye to all he knew. God promised him unbelievable things; he trusted and believed God for His promises, and they came to pass. Abraham, father of many nations, through whom all the nations of the world have been blessed, is held up throughout history as the person of faith. If I am, through faith, a descendant of Abraham, then I cannot escape the wrestling questions: What does it mean to go further, to launch out into the deep, to surrender to something that is as yet unknown? What does it mean to, Abraham-like, leave the 'country' I have known, my kinsfolk and my father's house, and go? What does it mean to risk all that has been accomplished, all the precious affirmations and securities, to shake myself free and set out? What does it mean to leave behind the safety of lifelong ways of coping, the well-ordered, locked-away emotions, the drip-feed of pain and joy that my flesh would tell me is all that I could stand? What does it mean to enter a new world where all is not known, where much is mystery, where the challenges are great, and the rewards not visible, or easily attainable, where all I cling to is a promise from a Voice still barely heard, that there are treasures hidden in the darkness, riches stored in secret places, and the only way to find them is to go?

Years ago, I studied for two years at the University of Toronto in Canada. I was on a Commonwealth Scholarship, which meant that during that time I was not permitted to come home, but rather, in the intervening summer, had to learn more about my host country, along with doing something connected with my course, which was in Community Development. I eventually arranged to work on a pilot project in Vancouver's Skid Row with thirty other young people from all over Canada. Because the Social Work term finished later than others, I had to travel out on my own. I decided to go by train and it was quite an adventure. It took rather longer than scheduled because of forest fires in Northern Ontario. We travelled, it seemed, forever through Ontario, and on into the Prairies, where the land stretched flat as far as the eye could see, without a single bump or hillock until we reached the foothills of the Rockies. The whole train-crew changed at Edmonton, and some fond farewells were said to friendships that had been struck up on the first stage of the trip. The next stage was a breathtaking journey through the mountains. If you sat in the dome-car as the train snaked its way around cliffs, or hugged the edge of mighty rivers, you could see the back carriages running almost parallel as we twisted and turned. On and on, until at last we began the approach to quieter things and the final lap.

It was only on this last stage that my anxiety-level about my destination started to rise. It had all been so fascinating up until then, but now I began really to worry. Someone had told me that the central train station in Vancouver was not in a very desirable area of the city. Because of the delay, we were arriving well after our stated time. It was late at night and I didn't know anyone. I was on my own. Who would meet me? How would I get safely to my final destination, and if and when I did get there, what would they be like – this community to whom I had already committed myself for three months? The train pulled in slowly. Feeling very apprehensive, I gathered my luggage together (I always take too much), and began to step out onto the platform. Before both feet had touched the ground, a pair of arms went round me, someone kissed me on the cheek, and a chorus of voices rang out, 'Welcome to the Inner City.' The other project members, including the leader, had met every train coming west for the previous day and a half, in the hopes that I'd be on one of them, and all was well!

From time to time, the memory of that trip comes back to me very vividly. It seems to me like a little video of the journey of life, with its encouragements and hindrances, its ordinary and extraordinary, its hellos and goodbyes, the flat times when life just jogs along and nothing much seems to happen, the heights and the depths, until as we get older and reach the final lap, the enormity of what's up ahead begins to dawn on us. Maybe the anxiety level and the doubts arise. We wonder about the final destination, 'What will it be like? Who will meet me? Will I even be able to get off the train, so weighed down am I with unnecessary baggage? Will I be recognised and welcomed? Will I be able to find my own way home? Will it even feel like home?'

Whatever our questions, our fears, our apprehensions, this is one journey we all have to make. When I was a child, and an adolescent, and in my twenties, someone in their fifties seemed absolutely ancient – one foot in the grave! Now in my fifties, there is still within me that child, that adolescent, that girl in her twenties. I don't 'feel' in my fifties (whatever that feeling is meant to be like), and the way ahead is still as beckoning and alluring and challenging and scary and exciting (or more so) as it was all those years ago. This body, this 'house' I live in, may not be able to do as much as it once did, but the essence of who I am is still on pilgrimage. I love that little verse hidden away in the middle of Hebrews Chapter 11: 'It was by faith that Jacob when he was old and dying, blessed each of Joseph's sons, and bowed in worship as he leaned on his staff' (Heb 11:21). What a fascinating picture of an old man who had lived a very earthy, intermittently faithful life, albeit with a very honest relationship with his God, coming to the end of his days, still travelling, still with his staff, still worshipping, still looking forward to the place beyond the end!

On the journey, what can we do, how can we live, so that when we are approaching the destination, we can be on tiptoe in expectancy rather than curled up in fear, anxiety, loneliness or denial? How do we prepare ourselves for the final welcome of death, for the end that is the beginning? It seems to me that we need to recognise again, or maybe for the first time, that we, too, are a pilgrim people, nomads like Abraham, continually called to leave certain things behind and to move on, uncluttered, with God. The people of faith in the Bible were like that. The psalmist says 'I am your guest, a traveller passing through as my ancestors were before me' (Ps 39). In Hebrews Chapter 11 the writer pauses in the middle of the great roll-call of faith to say, 'All these faithful ones died without receiving what God had promised them, but they saw it all from a distance and welcomed the promises of God. They agreed that they were no more than foreigners and nomads on earth. And obviously people who talk like that are looking forward to a country they can call their own. If they had meant the country they came from, they would have found a way to go back. But they were looking for a better place, a heavenly homeland. That is why God is not ashamed to be called their God, for he has prepared a heavenly city for them' (Heb 11:13-16).

One thing about being a pilgrim is that you can't carry too much baggage. It prevents you travelling too far. You get cluttered up and eventually settle down and don't see life or faith as a journey any more. We don't just carry physical baggage. We don't merely hoard things, we also store up old fears, resentments, bitterness, unforgiveness, worries, anger, loneliness. As we get older, instead of being thrown out, these can become precious treasures that we take out, count, gloat over, and put away again because, perhaps, they provide us with a sort of negative security and identity. We wouldn't know who we were without them. How much better to discard, to do a periodic spring-clean, to go to the dump – with God – and to be able to move on to new things with a lighter spirit, a spirit that has more energy and alertness for the journey, because it is not so weighed down. And to trust; pilgrims need to trust, even when they can't see the way ahead. They need to trust that, even when the journey is in darkness and seeming confusion, there is a destination and they will get there. And when they take the time to listen, to cultivate that trust, to pray, there comes to the perceptive pilgrim, at first like a faint drumbeat, the sense that their destination seems vaguely recognisable, that somehow, some way, they are getting fleeting glimpses of familiar territory, that the farther they travel, the stronger their memory, a memory that is beyond memory of home. As people of faith, we believe that we have come from God and that we are going back to God, travelling home. To trust that God knows the end from the beginning, that all things are in His hands, that even when it doesn't seem like it, He does all things well, is a prerequisite for setting out as pilgrims to the place beyond the end where we will know ourselves at home.

CHAPTER TWO

VIEWING POINTS AND RESTING PLACES

But is there for the night a resting place?
A roof for when the slow dark hours begin.

— Christina Rosetti, 'Up-Hill'[1]

On any journey, resting places are vital; call them inns, or cities of refuge, or oases, or places apart – somewhere where the spirit can be refreshed, the soul revived, the body renewed. In a world where busyness predominates, these places become increasingly special and precious. Looking back, I see my life punctuated with them, each important at a particular stage. But the one that has been enduring, since before I can remember, has been Donegal; in particular, the extreme northwest in all its rugged beauty, its ever-changing sea and sky, the miles of golden sand, the heather and the rocks, and the constant reassuring presence of Muckish mountain. As a child I used to think that it followed us around, changing shape as it went, but still recognisable and solidly there, like a protective, ageing relative. Even when it couldn't be seen, when the mists came down or the rain fell heavily, you still knew, you believed, it was there, that it would never let you down.

Because my father was a clergyman, as a family we moved about quite a bit. The one fixed point in our lives was Donegal, where generations of Pattersons had farmed the rocky land of Cloonmass on Sheephaven Bay. When he was first a minister, there was no such

---

1. Alfred H. Miles, ed., *Rosetti to Tynan* (London: George Routledge & Sons Ltd, 1907), p. 18.

thing as a minimum salary for Presbyterian clergy. We were not at all well off – in fact, quite the reverse. My mother, as a medical doctor, subsidised the family income by doing locum work for other doctors, and so we managed. But whatever else happened or didn't happen, there was always a summer holiday, back to the roots, to Cloonmass in Donegal for one glorious carefree month. It was the one time in the year, apart from Christmas, that held great excitement and wonder for us as children. Weeks before we were due to go, the large tin trunk was pulled out and left open, and everyone put in what they wanted. It sat there surrounded by a sense of expectancy, even of magic. It symbolised all that was life-giving and free and joyous in our lives.

As I look back over the years I remember good weather, sunny days, long summer evenings, echoes across still waters, starry nights, the sense of awe at spring tides, the distinctive smell of turf-smoke hanging on the air, wheaten bread baked expertly in the pot-oven by my mother, freshly caught mackerel from the bay grilled for breakfast, morning and evening treks to the home farm for milk, a cow called Violet. I recall evenings around the fire, my father telling stories of his childhood in Donegal, my brother leading a sing-song from a wealth of Irish folk music. He always knew the tunes, while I had a facility for remembering words; my mother and my sister could sing, so together we put on a presentable performance, even when there was no other audience to hear. There were days when there weren't enough hours to pack in all the swimming, cycling, walking and picnics. I'd go to sleep with the sounds of bleating sheep and waves breaking on the shore. I used to long for the month to last forever, but it never did. The packing up, the going back, the busyness of a manse family all took over, but on Christmas Day some precious pieces of turf, saved from the summer, were placed ceremoniously on the fire and, when one of them was smouldering enough, my mother would lift it out with the tongs, and waft the smoke around the room. 'Close your eyes and you're in Donegal', she would say. And we did; and for one glorious moment we were!

Places become special for all sorts of reasons, usually because of happy memories. But some have something extra still, and Donegal is one of them. Perhaps it is sacred space. For me, it is a threshold place, as if I'm standing on tiptoe in expectancy, a place of the third dimension, where I can almost reach out and touch the eternal. My father, writing once about his fellow countrymen, said, 'Donegal people speak quietly like the Scottish Highlanders. There is much to make them lower their voices. In the midst of the everlasting strength and beauty of the hills, and always in the presence of a mystery about to be revealed, how can they raise their voices? There is so much to keep a man quiet.'

When I was first a student, another oasis place was the island of Iona. The introduction to Iona came through my involvement with the Presbyterian Community Centre at Queen's University, Belfast, where I studied for my first degree. The Centre was an amazing place, largely because of the charismatic leadership of its chaplain, Ray Davey. During his many years there it was rarely known by its official title, but simply as 'Ray's'. Generations of students have been challenged and inspired in the whole area of community, and specifically of Christian community, through his leadership and example, not only as a student chaplain, but as the founder and first Director of Corrymeela, now so well known for its work for reconciliation and peace. Ray often used to remind us that Jesus never said, 'Blessed are the peace-lovers', but rather 'Blessed are the peacemakers'. Throughout the years since then, I have learnt, at least a little, the truth of those words. The promise to the makers of peace is that they will be called children of God. Such friends of God are not always automatically welcomed in every quarter. To be a peacemaker can be a costly, messy business and almost always a lonely one. Little did we know, in those early years of the 1960s as young and enthusiastic students, how soon we would be challenged by such a calling.

Many visitors made their way to that Centre at Queen's. Among them was George MacLeod, a larger-than-life figure, founder of the Iona Community, someone who was always pushing out further the frontiers of what it meant to be Christian in the twentieth century. He had such a way with words, such conviction and boldness in his presentation, such a facility for seizing the moment, such impatience with much of the institutional red tape, that it was small wonder that people flocked to hear him and began to visit Iona, not only because of its holy places and its sense of mystery, but to encounter this most controversial figure who, at times, must have been quite a thorn in the flesh of the denomination that had nurtured him in the faith! For myself, when I read such words as the following, I could not but be convinced that here was something I needed to explore further.

> I am recovering the claim that Jesus was not crucified in a cathedral between two candles, but on a cross between two thieves, on the town garbage heap, at a crossroads so cosmopolitan that they had to write his title in Hebrew and in Latin and in Greek (or shall we say in English, in Bantu and in Afrikaans), at the kind of place where cynics talk and thieves curse and soldiers gamble. Because that is where he died. And it is what he died about. And that is where churchmen should be and what churchmanship should be about.[2]

---

2. George MacLeod, *Only One Way Left* (Glasgow: Iona Community, 1956), p. 38.

On a regular basis, Ray took groups of students on pilgrimage to
Iona. One visit, and I was 'caught'. Partly because of the strong links
with Ireland and with that fiery, earthy saint, Columba, partly
because of George MacLeod, partly because there was that sense of
being on tiptoe, this threshold place gripped me, and became for me
a source of refreshment and inspiration. There is an old prophecy
attributed to Columba:

> *In Iona of my heart, Iona of my love,*
> *Instead of monks' voices shall be lowing of cattle,*
> *But ere the world come to an end*
> *Iona shall be as it was.* [3]

With Iona Community members increasingly scattered all over the
world, many in coal-face ministries, seeking to bear witness to what
'churchmen' should be about, perhaps this prophecy was beginning
to be fulfilled?

For several years, a summer was never complete without my
spending some weeks on the island doing whatever came to hand –
leading youth camps, assisting in the kitchen, rejoicing in being part
of that communal life which, while geographically seeming so remote
from the heartbeats of the world, somehow appeared to be in the
mainstream of what God was doing.

And through it all, there was that deep sense of God. As I look
back, yes, I remember the people, the lively discussions, the fun, the
traditional Scottish dances in the village hall, the concerts in the
Abbey refectory, the weekly pilgrimages around the island; but most
of all, I remember the bell ringing in the Abbey calling us to morning

---

3. Quoted in E. Mairi MacArthur, *Columba's Island* (Edinburgh: Edinburgh
University Press, 1995), p. 45.

and evening prayer, the sense of the holy all around, and the deep peace that pervaded everything, even in the fiercest storm. The Celtic blessing by Fiona MacLeod encapsulates this for me:

> *Deep peace of the running wave to you.*
> *Deep peace of the flowing air to you.*
> *Deep peace of the quiet earth to you.*
> *Deep peace of the shining star to you.*
> *Deep peace of the Son of Peace to you.* [4]

Over the years of trouble in Ireland, it was hard to keep hope alive as initiative after initiative on the political front failed and violence increased. They failed, primarily, because there was no change in attitude. Attitudes are about minds and hearts. Until there is some movement there, there is not going to be much progress. Attitudes are changed eventually by the building of relationships, by a willingness to be open and vulnerable, by inviting someone who is different across the threshold of one's life, and to risk enough also to step across theirs. In this there is no quick fix, only years of keeping on keeping on. As relationships have become established and have been nurtured, I have found an increasing number of resting places, a roof for when the slow dark hours begin.

I remember in the mid 1980s realising that many people in the South of Ireland had never been to the North, and vice versa; also that when people in the South heard the name 'Presbyterian', there was a tendency to lump us all together as having a particular political viewpoint and hardness of attitude. So I decided to take a tour around the South with a friend and, instead of staying in hotels or guesthouses, to stay in monasteries and convents. We hoped that as

---

4. Quoted in David Adam, *The Open Gate* (London: Triangle/SPCK, 1994), p. 113.

we made connections and built relationships with people, the next time they saw certain news reports on television, they wouldn't tar everyone with the one brush but would think of two individuals whom they had met. We started out with the Sacred Heart Sisters in Tallaght in Dublin, and then moved to the Cistercian Monastery at Mount Melleray. On the first evening we made our way to the guesthouse for a meal, and found ourselves seated at a table with several people from different parts of Ireland. There was the usual polite exchange of names and comments on the weather. Someone asked us where we were going. On hearing this, one young man leant across the table and said, 'It's well for these nuns that can get cheap accommodation!' My friend leant forward and replied, 'Actually, Ruth is a Presbyterian minister.' There was a silence that seemed to last for about five minutes, although in reality it was only seconds. And then everyone began to talk at a much deeper level and the conversation flowed.

From Mount Melleray we moved on to the Carmelite Friars at Kinsale, and then out to one of the most southwesterly tips of Ireland, Ballinskelligs, to the holiday home of the Presentation Sisters of Cork and Kerry. After four unforgettable days of appalling weather and wonderful hospitality we moved up to County Clare, to the Mercy Sisters in Ennistymon. We happened to arrive on a Saturday evening. The convent was situated next door to the church and the presbytery. The local curate must have heard news of our visit because, within an hour of our arrival, I received a phone call from him asking if I would give the homily at Mass the next morning. I replied hesitantly, 'Well, I'd prefer not to; I'm on holiday.' My friend was jumping up and down beside the telephone, mouthing the words 'Say yes!' So I said 'Yes!' Next morning we entered a large and crowded church. I am quite sure that very few of the congregation would ever have laid eyes on a Presbyterian before.

The way the curate introduced us was as follows, 'I'm sure most of you think Protestants have horns! Well, there are two here today to prove that they haven't!' As I was walking out to the lectern to deliver the homily, these words of inspiration from our friendly curate, who was trying, not very effectively, to keep his voice at a stage whisper, were ringing in my ears, 'Keep it short! It's the semi-finals in Thurles!'

Reluctantly leaving Ennistymon, we made our way to Connemara, to the Benedictine Community at Kylemore Abbey, before turning the car homewards, tired but satisfied. The trip had worked. All these years later, those relationships have held and been nurtured. They, in turn, have led to other friendships, and have created a network of people around the country, who, while having different interests, traditions and sometimes language, are growing in their recognition of their primary allegiance and, therefore, of their togetherness in Jesus.

Resting places are often also viewing points. Across the Back Strand from Cloonmass in County Donegal is Ards Forest Park. At low tide it is possible to cross over and walk for several hours along wooded paths and over headlands, before the returning tide makes wading back impossible. At frequent intervals on such forest walks there are magnificent viewing points. I have often been walking for long stretches through the enchanting gloom created by the seemingly unending stretches of fir trees, only to step out suddenly into a clearing, where I am able to see where I've come from and where I'm going. Or else I come across a wooden signpost indicating a viewing point, which, if followed, very soon opens out vistas of incredible beauty and vastness.

On the side of the mountain that rises up behind Kylemore Abbey in Connemara, there is a statue. I'm not very 'into' statues, but this particular one speaks to me quite powerfully. Well, it doesn't 'speak' exactly, or move, or weep, but there is something about it that has an important message. It is, if you like, another viewing point for me. It's a statue of Jesus, a Sacred Heart statue, bigger than life-size. Even down at the Abbey or by the lake, you can look up and see it clearly, a white figure against the browns and greens and greys of the mountainside. But if you are energetic enough to make the climb you will find a very weatherbeaten figure, a strong figure, 'nice' as statues go, with his arms outstretched, gazing over vast parts of Ireland. On a clear day Achill Island is visible to the west, with the Atlantic Ocean stretching as far as the eye can see. On every other side are the hills and mountains and valleys of the Ireland that, in some sense, whatever part of it we come from, we claim as ours. If you look more closely, you will see that one hand of this figure, the left one, has been broken off, either through vandalism or by the elements. The arms, however, are still reaching out, and the right hand is intact. The figure, though battered, is strong. It has endured the fiercest of gales, the most turbulent of storms, and still it stands, reaching out, perhaps in blessing, perhaps in entreaty. For me, it is an image of Jesus as His heart aches and breaks over what is happening in this small island that has such potential to be a witness for Him.

Whenever I climb up, there are two thoughts that come to me. Firstly, it is as if the broken-off hand symbolises the disunity of the Church – the broken body is incomplete. How can the world, how can Ireland be blessed, if the two hands are not together lifted up in benediction, if they are not together inviting weary ones to come and rest? It is as if Jesus, to whom all power in heaven and on earth has been given, is looking out over Ireland in vulnerability and brokenness, 'limited' because He chooses to work through us, and we have broken what was united, so we, His Church, are ineffective because we are living and working at half-power.

The second thought is that here is no pathetic figure. Yes, the left hand, the hand the warrior would use to hold the shield of protection, has been broken off, but the right hand is intact — symbolic of power, authority and victory. Yes, maybe the shield of protection has been lowered at the moment, and the festering and turmoil of the centuries have come to the surface, leaving gaping wounds in a people who have not yet fully bowed the knee and yielded submission to their rightful King. But the Lord is still in control, the victory belongs to Him, the right hand is intact, and His faithfulness endures. I am reminded of the words of the psalmist:

The strong right arm of the Lord is raised in triumph.
The strong right arm of the Lord has done glorious things!
I will not die, but I will live
To tell what the Lord has done.
(Psalm 118:16-17)

It is, for me, a little picture of hope. When hope flickers and falters, weariness increases, energy fails, and the journey becomes more difficult. Yet, deep within, perhaps only at times a faint whisper, there is something that tells us that we must keep going, that we must keep hope alive against all possible odds, that even when things are at their darkest, we must continue to fling the affirmation of faith against the darkness. This is not a naive optimism, but rather the hope that comes from knowing, beyond everything, that God is not divorced from what has been happening in Ireland or from any situation. He is present, He knows the plans He has for us, and those plans are for good.

There have been other important viewing points on the journey so far that have not been places at all, but rather movements of people. One was the Charismatic Movement. It seems to me that it is no coincidence that Charismatic Renewal in Ireland is roughly the same age as the current Troubles. I find that an awesome and a sobering thought; that hand-in-hand with the nightmare of recent years, there has been this mighty move of the Spirit. Where would we have been without it, without God the Holy Spirit leading so many into a deeper and more intimate relationship with Jesus? Where would we have been without Him – nurturing gifts, healing, challenging, blessing, training us in the weapons of spiritual warfare, empowering people to walk through valleys of darkness, and to emerge, not with less but with more – more faith, more love, more forgiveness; and perhaps most significantly, breaking down the human-made barriers of culture, tradition and denomination. Parallel with the bombing, killing and destruction, with the flowering of the weeds of sectarianism, bigotry, unforgiveness, hatred and fear, God the Holy Spirit was planting another garden, the fruits of which, we hoped, would be evident for the world to see.

But somehow, somewhere, something went wrong. Why did more not happen? A few of the fruits became signs of hope for other places. Many other fruits remained hidden, though nonetheless significant. But why did we not see more victories for love, forgiveness, peace, unity? We prayed the prayer 'Come Holy Spirit'. We believed. So what was it? Why has the night been so long, and the road at times too hard?

On reflection, I believe that part of what happened was that the Holy Spirit was true to His work. He came as renewer, as life-giver, as comforter, and there was a glorious honeymoon period. But He cannot dwell where there is rubbish, and so, after the initial visitation, He began His disturbing work, His spring-cleaning work. People began to discover areas in their lives that they had previously ignored or repressed – old wounds, old bigotries, old sins. The Spirit was bringing these to the surface, not to taunt us, but so that we might be healed. Some had the courage and the faith to go on such a journey. But others, maybe because we did not have enough wise, mature leadership, or maybe because we did not want to face the pain of what was coming, pushed it back down again, and put the lid firmly on it. So we were left, in many instances, with a movement that, while being life-giving and effective to a certain extent, was, by and large, more superficial than God intended. The repressed baggage of recent years and of centuries past did not go away, but rather festered and spread, becoming more firmly rooted in our communal psyche.

Through the years, these two unlikely travelling companions – communal violence and charismatic renewal – have both tended to become institutionalised, leaving us, as we stand on the brink of a new day, with an almost tougher job to face than thirty years previously. While there have been major breakthroughs in certain relationships, there is still a silent scream rising from the depths of so many wounded, sinned against and sinning individuals, and a silent scream rising from the heart of Ireland itself that carries all the searing pain of centuries. It all needs to be voiced and heard, with all that that implies of really listening, of the costly seeking after truth, of letting go, repenting, forgiving, reconciling. So, we need to pray again, 'Come Holy Spirit', this time to the Holy Spirit the Paraclete, the One who answers the cry. This 'viewing point', with such a vista, calls me to dare to be open to the Spirit in ways that hitherto I have resisted, to be prepared to go farther than I have ever gone before.

There have also been people who, at various stages of the journey, have gifted me with new horizons, with a wider expanse of view and fresh courage for the pilgrimage. Apart from those already referred to, I will only mention two out of the many whom I believe Jesus arranged to join me on the road, especially at the times when fresh vision was necessary, or when it did not seem that I could take another step forward, so hard had the way become.

One such was Tullio Vinay, who died in 1996, a pastor in the Waldensian Church in Italy. During the Second World War he helped many Jews in Italy to escape from the Nazis. When the war was over, there was so much devastation, hatred, division and disillusionment that he decided something had to be done. He built a village in the Italian Alps called Agape, to which people, especially young people from all over Europe, could come and begin to find hope and healing, to build bridges and to restore some of the waste places in their lives. When this work was well established, he then looked around to find one of the worst slums in Europe, where he could go with a small community of people and live, in an effort, as he put it, to make the new world of Jesus Christ a reality. He found that slum in a town called Riesi in the centre of Sicily. There, people lived as they had lived for centuries, in medieval poverty and squalor, under the fearful control of the Mafia. He called this project Servizio Cristiano. He lived there until ill-health and old age compelled him to leave.

I never visited Riesi but as a student in the early sixties I ran a little support group for Vinay's work at Queen's. His visits to Ireland were always memorable, and it was fitting that he was the one chosen by Ray Davey to open the new Corrymeela Centre in 1965. To be in his presence, to hear him speak and to know that he had underwritten his words with his life was an inspiration. For me, in his person, he was a viewing point, a gift from God. I remember him once describing his vision of a new Riesi in these words: 'They shall build houses together and go into them singing with their children. Together shall they work and feed those who are in need. Then, at evening, they shall come out of their homes and move together towards the assembly place and say, "Our Father who art in Heaven...".' It could be a vision for a new Ireland.

When I was working on the chaplaincy team at Queen's, Jean Vanier – founder of the L'Arche communities for people with learning disabilities, and co-founder, along with Marie-Helène Mathieu, of Faith and Light – paid his first visit to Belfast. I had read one of his books, and heard a lot about him, both in Canada and at home, and decided to go and listen to what he had to say. He spoke about forgiveness. I still remember the impact of that message, and how powerful yet gentle his word and his person were. I felt I had to go and talk with him, to make connection. I recall pushing my way up to the front through a crowd of people, till I found myself standing in front of him. Once there, shyness overcame me, and all I could say was, 'Thank you', before hurriedly leaving the hall!

Many, many years later, in 1994, I was asked to be part of a planning team to bring Jean Vanier to Northern Ireland for a Festival of Faith and Friendship, entitled 'Healing our Brokenness'. It took place in June 1995 at the University of Ulster, Coleraine, during the first ceasefire. To listen to Jean is to listen to someone who has truly found his resting place in Jesus, and who has the humility, the ability, the gentleness and the passion to point others beyond himself to their true resting place also. At Coleraine, people of all ages, backgrounds and denominations, people with learning disabilities, people who had experienced so much suffering, all found a safe place to tell their story, to discover new friends and to express their faith.

Out of that Festival, encouraged by Jean, another little movement was born – Faith and Friendship – to bring together people from different religious traditions to discover what they can give to each other and what they can receive from each other. There are now five little groups in the North, whose members, drawn from the different traditions, feel able to tell their story, to discover difference in an atmosphere of respect, to recognise unity in diversity, to share their faith experience and to deepen their friendship.

Jean became and continues to be for me a 'viewing point' and a most faithful pilgrim on the journey. It strikes me very forcibly that he and the movements of L'Arche and Faith and Light have a prophetic voice for Ireland, and indeed for the world. In these two movements, it is the people with disabilities, the poor, the little and the broken, who are special, and who show us the truth about ourselves. That truth is that we are all such as these – poor, little, broken, but also the beloved of Jesus. Ireland has a rich Christian heritage, but it is also little, broken and divided, handicapped by its past. It is a place of anguish, a trouble spot that never seems to learn. So easily it could be written off. But it is also, I believe, a seedbed of hope. Ireland, precisely because of what it has been through, still has the chance to show the world the truth about itself, namely that the whole world is poor, broken and divided, but is also the beloved. In the security of discovering ourselves to be loved, we can begin to build relationships across the broken places in an atmosphere grounded in faith, expressed in friendship and nurtured by the Spirit. Jean has reminded us often that community is founded on forgiveness and builds itself up through love. He has also clearly underlined for us the importance of the little, and of an all-powerful, all-loving God who chose to act in littleness to save a big world that He loves. Both of these truths are vital for the Church in all its branches, and for Ireland as a whole. They are also crucially important for me, as is his constant encouragement to seek my true resting place in Jesus.

CHAPTER THREE

CROSSROADS

I shall be telling this with a sigh
Somewhere ages and ages hence:
Two roads diverged in a wood, and I —
I took the one less travelled by,
And that has made all the difference.
　　　　　　　— Robert Frost, 'The Road Not Taken'[1]

On any journey there will be a turning point, other roads will beckon and there certainly will be crossroads, maybe many of them. My journey has had its fair share of them, and I expect there will be many more before it's over.

I remember very vividly on one particular day in January 1966 receiving two communications presenting me with a stark choice. I had completed a BA at Queen's, and was in the middle of a social work diploma year. On that morning I received a telegram offering me a Commonwealth Scholarship to Canada to any university of my choice to do a Master's Degree in Social Work, and half an hour later a letter telling me that I had been accepted for Voluntary Service Overseas. What to do? In the words of Robert Frost again,

Both that morning equally lay
In leaves no step had trodden black.[2]

---

1. Robert Frost, *Complete Poems of Robert Frost* (New York: Holt, Reinhart and Winston, 1949), p. 131.
2. Ibid.

After some agonising, I decided to opt for Canada. I felt that the opportunity to work overseas might come again, but the chance to do such a course, specialising in community development, was a one-off. At that stage there was no such course in the British Isles. The only places were Holland, Canada or the United States. For me it was to prove the first of several roads less travelled by. So at the age of twenty-one, in 1966, I set off for a strange land, a different culture. I remember the stretching of adjustment, the widening of horizons, as I studied and worked with fellow students from many different countries and, in that first year especially, I recall my field-work placement. Out of about ninety students, seven had elected to do community development, it being a relatively new option. I was placed along with another girl in a Reformed Jewish synagogue in North Toronto called Holy Blossom Temple. After a week my companion requested a replacement, and I was left as the only non-Jewish person, so green in many ways, in this strange environment! On reflection, after a somewhat shaky start, it was a most enriching and rewarding experience, one that served to deepen the immense regard and respect I had for the Jewish people.

One of the first, seemingly innocuous tasks allotted to me was to order a luncheon for the directors of the synagogue, who were meeting on a particular Sunday. I duly did so, and on the Sunday morning was sitting having breakfast in the college where I was staying, when a fellow resident said, 'Well, this is your big day. What did you order for their lunch?' I was about to reply when I happened to look down at what I was eating for breakfast – bacon! 'Ham sandwiches,' I replied, outwardly groaning and inwardly panicking. I left immediately and walked the streets until I found a delicatessen that was open early on a Sunday, bought up all the suitable sandwiches I could see, arrived at the synagogue before my supervisor, and did a quick swap around. All was well, and the other residents on my floor feasted on ham sandwiches that evening! I did not report my faux pas to my superior until the end of the year, when we laughed together over it. But for the next few months my door in the college bore a sticker with the words, 'The world's greatest ham!'

I loved Canada – the way of life, the sense of a country that was still 'young' with all sorts of opportunities, in particular the chance to develop one's chosen field of work relatively early in life. The intervening summer, working in Vancouver, rounded off with a three-week camping trip to Quebec, Nova Scotia and Prince Edward Island, gave me a further sense of the vastness and beauty of the land. In my second year I moved into Yorkville, the then hippie area of Toronto, and lived with a friend from the summer project in an attic apartment above an antiques shop. What a time to be a student, the mid-sixties, with all the questioning of structures, the deep social awareness, the anti-war movements – and the music! Had I stayed another year, I might have remained in Canada for good, putting down roots, as one does, in one's early twenties. But during that second year I came to yet another crossroads. Ray Davey, still chaplain at Queen's, wrote in early 1968 asking me to come back and be his assistant on the chaplaincy team. He had always had a female assistant, and theological qualifications weren't essential. I declined. He wrote again, and I declined again. On the third time of writing, I felt someone was trying to tell me something, and I accepted. None of us knew then what the autumn of 1968 at Queen's and the subsequent years would bring to life in Northern Ireland.

Looking back now to those two years, certain things crowd into my memory. Toronto winters with some amazing ice-storms, Christmas and Thanksgiving spent with a family in Lindsay, Ontario, long conversations with good friends sitting on the back doorstep of the disused church that was home to us for the summer on

Vancouver's Skid Row, some stimulating and exciting classwork, standing outside Toronto City Hall with thousands of others the day after the assassination of Martin Luther King Jr, listening to one of his favourite songs, scarcely able to believe he was gone. For me, his was one of the voices of inspiration in those years, and even today certain words of his have the same ring of truth and the same power to galvanise into action as they had then. He said once that it was not possible to like everyone, because liking was a natural reaction, but that it was possible to love everyone, even one's enemies, if loving implied 'understanding creative, redemptive goodwill toward all men'.[3] And it seems to me, so many years later, that that is still a vital key for moving any peace process forward, even in Ireland!

What can I say about those years at Queen's, which began in the heady exhilarating autumn of 1968, when we believed that we were working for a better Ireland and a better world. There was such a sense of life and so much togetherness in those early days. But Queen's being largely a home-based university, was like a microcosm of the wider community, and so what we saw unfolding in the subsequent months and years was largely a reflection of what was happening in the community as a whole.

Working among students, the most important thing for me was the establishing of relationships, across whatever divide, be it sectarian, political, or plain lack of interest in anything associated with the label of Church or religion. What I experienced during those three years only served to reinforce a conviction that had been growing through my early student years and my time in Canada — that the Church, if it was to mean anything, had to be involved where people were living out their lives, where they worked (or didn't

---

3. Martin Luther King, *The Trumpet of Conscience* (London: Hodder and Stoughton, 1967), p. 88.

work), where they sweated and suffered, not divorced from reality in some holy huddle, however well-meaning, worthy and good. Along with that was an equally firm conviction that religious denomination was not overly important to the people among whom I had lived and worked, but that there was still an interest and a positive questioning about Christianity, about who Jesus was and is, and a very real search for purpose and meaning.

I remember when I was eight years old, playing on my own in a little park in a seaside town in County Down, when I was suddenly joined by an unknown and quite aggressive ten-year-old. Out of the blue, she fired at me the unheard-of question, 'Are you a Catholic or a Protestant?' I didn't really know what she meant, but I knew that whatever it was she was asking jarred with me, and, although quite timid, I drew myself up to my full height (which wasn't very tall), and said with as much dignity as I could muster, 'I'm neither of those things. I'm a Presbyterian!'

Many years later I could still respond, 'I'm neither of those things'. What do I mean by that? I don't mean that I reject the tradition into which I was born, nor do I mean that I become all things to all people, but I do mean that I have an identity that transcends all the other identities or labels, and that identity is Christian – one of Christ's ones. It's so crucial for me to keep that primary identity in focus in a situation like Northern Ireland or any situation where people (myself included) would seek to lock themselves into self-made or inherited prisons of prejudice or fear or ignorance or unforgiveness. I cannot even begin to set out on the journey, let alone seek to walk the reconciliation road, unless I am constantly reminded of who I am in Jesus.

I can recall very clearly the first gunfire I heard in Belfast in 1969, sitting on the edge of my bed, asking myself, as I'm sure so many others were doing at the time, 'Can this be our city? What is happening to us?' For those with any sense of concern about what was going on, or thrust into involvement because they had no choice, life was lived at a very intense level, all the time. It wasn't that we were too consciously aware of the intensity, but when, for example, I drove to Dublin or Donegal, or went further afield, there was always the sense of a subconscious relaxation, or a letting go, which immediately tightened up again upon return, as if we were holding ourselves in readiness for the next shocking event. People in Northern Ireland have lived like that for thirty years. Is it any wonder that now there is such a communal weariness and, by and large, such a yearning for peace?

As my contract at Queen's was nearing an end, another crossroads was looming. Having lived fully every moment of those eventful three years, it did not seem right to have it renewed. A change was in order. What to do? By now community work was becoming the 'in' word. I started applying for jobs. One day, I received an offer of a community development post working with women and children in Belfast. Reading the letter, I had the dawning realisation that this was not what was being asked of me. A thought, which must have been swimming around in my subconscious for some time, suddenly burst into consciousness; it was like a flash of recognition. 'I want to study theology', the inner voice insisted. Rather than be ungracious to those who had offered me the post, I decided to go and explain myself in person. When I had finished, there was silence. So I turned to the director and said, 'Well, I suppose this means I'm committing suicide as regards a professional career in community development?' 'Yes', he replied, 'You are.'

I remember walking downstairs and out on to the street, overwhelmed with self-doubt and apprehension. 'What have you done?' was the persistent question, to which there was then no answer. Later, when called upon to explain myself, not once but many times, all I could say was that personally I felt that to study theology would make sense of much that I had done previously, and that I believed that there was a need for some people in Northern Ireland who were trained not only in community work or theology, but who could combine both in themselves because of the particular nature of what was happening to us. At the same time, I decided to seek to become a candidate for ordination within the Presbyterian Church in Ireland, knowing that at that point no denomination in Ireland accepted the concept of ordained women. Ordination then was for me a secondary aim. To study theology was the most important thing, and this I would have done had I never been accepted as a candidate for ordination. As it was, unknown to me, another woman was applying at the same time. Faced with two applications, the General Assembly of the Presbyterian Church decided to debate the issue. Meanwhile, I went ahead to Edinburgh University to study for a degree in theology. The only reason I happened to be out in front, testing the waters for the others, the first woman to be ordained, was because my fellow applicant, Joan Barr, waited for the Church's decision, whereas I felt I had to go ahead anyway. In 1972 the whole issue was debated, but the Assembly couldn't reach agreement. It was sent down to the then twenty-two presbyteries in Ireland to discuss and return their findings. They did so. Eighteen declared in favour, three against, and one confused. Sometimes I think that if we were faced with such a decision today, eighteen would declare themselves confused, so slowly do people open themselves up to change, and so threatened they can feel by difference. In 1973 the momentous decision was taken that women could be accepted as candidates for the ministry of the Presbyterian Church in Ireland on the same basis as men. However, as has been proven so often, the passing of a law, the taking of a decision, and the living or acting out of it are two very different things. I was ordained on 2 January 1976. That evening the worst storm of the winter blew outside. One clergyman remarked that it was a sign of Divine displeasure at what was happening!

Now there are more than twenty of us, and the other Protestant denominations followed; firstly, the Non-Subscribing Presbyterians, then the Methodists and then the Church of Ireland. It has never been particularly easy for the women.

The journey towards completeness within the Body of Christ is far from over, certainly as we know it within our denomination. In fact, at times it seems as if it has hardly even begun. It is a struggle. Having of necessity been closely involved over many years, it is clearer than ever to me, that the first necessity is to be open to the power and leading of God's Spirit, in order that we might be there for and with Him, in order that complete personhood in Christ might be set against all the forces that would seek to destroy or diminish His work in the world. It is possible, also, that we could become so obsessed with the struggle for completeness that we might miss the point of it all, which is certainly not to boost women as such, but rather that the Body of Christ be complete in the world; that we might declare Him in all His wholeness to a land and a world so broken, weary, wounded and divided.

There have been so many discussions, arguments and debates about whether or not women should be ordained, and what part women should play in the Church. These have all been well-rehearsed and are well known. They have provided ammunition for pro and anti lobbies. I have never been happy with any form of militant movement, or with labels, or with one group seeking to dominate another. But one thought process about this whole issue that I found helpful is in an overview of Creation, the Fall, and Redemption. In the beginning God created human beings, making them to be like Himself. He created them, male and female, and blessed them. Yet, somehow, man feels under threat; maybe he has done so since that beginning, where Eve is presented as the mother of all living, and where we see the unfolding of the role of woman in Creation and, subsequently, in Redemption. It is Eve who reaches up for the forbidden fruit, who reaches up to take to herself the authority of God the Creator. Adam, father of humankind, takes the fruit at the prompting of Eve. So it is the woman who takes the initiative and the authority over man. It is woman who takes over from God, and it is Adam who plays the subordinate part. In a sense, man also stands in the background when Jesus, the One who comes to save His people, appears. It is Mary, the woman, in her complete submission to the will and purpose of God, who becomes the mother of the One who is to bring the whole of creation back to God. Mary's 'yes' is the complete reversal of Eve's action. It is through woman that the Word is made flesh. And it is woman who meets the risen Lord, and is sent to tell the disciples the Good News. Women are the first heralds of the New Era. The sin of Eve has been overcome.

So there is a biblical understanding that portrays man, the male, as having very little part in the drama of the Fall and the Restoration; he is almost a spectator. If fundamentalists reject this approach, then they will be in the position of having to question seriously the Creation account of Genesis, and also the Virgin Birth.

No wonder that man feels under threat, a feeling that is expressed in many ways. If we could but see it, much opposition to women playing a larger part in the Church is psychological rather than theological. There is a tremendous inner healing needed in all of us – courage on the part of both men and women to turn and face our own brokenness (including our sexuality), those areas in which we have been most wounded. This is not to repress those things, but to walk through them, guided by the Holy Spirit to a wholeness within ourselves that will enable us to accept one another, to stand upright in the freedom that faith brings, truly sisters and brothers, facing the issues of our times as one.

So how has this particular aspect of the journey been for me since taking the road less travelled by? Looking back, there have been certain negative areas in my life that were highlighted or brought to the fore through this whole experience of call to ministry as a woman (in my case, the first one, which had its added pressures). I have had to look at myself through the hurts and rejection of others, more from within the Church than outside of it. These things could have served to imprison me further, or caused me to turn back. Instead, by the grace of God, they became open doors to areas of greater freedom and wholeness within myself, and a greater empathy with others whose way leads them through the dark ravine. In those first years I experienced a deep sense of isolation and aloneness, which served to nurture feelings of inadequacy, unworthiness and rejection – far more powerful and more subtle enemies than any opposition or attack from outside. I know, too, what it is to labour under continuous and relentless judgement from others, to have to accept that, on one level, whether I liked it or not, the whole question of the ordination of women in Ireland was being judged on how, initially, one person performed or failed to perform. That brought me face-to-face with another dilemma; was I to strive, and necessarily fail, to achieve an impossible perfection in the eyes of men? Was I to become imprisoned by what others thought of me or expected from me? And what was I to do with the steady undermining through remarks, letters, tracts, phone calls, insinuations, all small in themselves, but adding up to a deep pit of hurt? Would they build up into a spirit of unforgiveness or bitterness, or was I going to be able to say, with understanding and compassion, from my heart, 'Well, God bless you!' All of these problems, and many others, were overshadowed by perhaps the most dangerous one of all, namely that of beginning to see oneself as a martyr, Elijah-like in her sense of being misunderstood, unaccepted, even persecuted. I am deeply thankful for a sense of humour. I remember one day waiting for a long time at the entrance to a hospital ward, having requested permission to visit a patient. While I waited, at least four male clergy walked past, unaccosted, did their visits, and left! Eventually I overheard a nurse say to the sister-in-charge, 'There's a girl outside says she's a minister!'

It seems that I am always only at the beginning of tapping into that deep sense of joy that comes from learning to walk, however stumblingly, the path of humility and obedience. But I have learnt, in ways that I can never forget, that I have no right to proclaim the Word, unless I first allow that Word to speak to me; that I have no right to minister, unless I am open enough to allow myself to be ministered to. I am discovering in a deeper and deeper way the importance of the body. I've had to allow pride to be dealt with, letting my brokenness be seen by people who have been willing to stand with me. And through it all there has been growing within me a new sense of my own worth, which stems not from anything I may achieve, but out of a deepening relationship with Jesus, a relationship that gives me a new identity, which is my true identity, the Ruth that God had in mind from the very beginning. I can thank Him today for the journey so far, even or maybe especially for the hardest times, for it has been in the facing of these through the power of the Holy Spirit that I know a little about the road to freedom. I also know that what He has done already is only a foretaste of what is to come. No matter what happens in terms of human decisions, the best is yet to be. God hasn't finished with any of us yet.

People often used to say to me, 'Surely the road to ordination was the most difficult part of that whole time?' And I would reply, 'No. No, it wasn't.' In Presbyterianism, a local congregation has to call or invite a person to be their minister, and that person should receive at least two-thirds of the votes from their full membership. The real testing point was whether there be a congregation brave enough (or foolish enough!) to call the first woman. I had to wait longer than most of my male colleagues, but eventually, in the autumn of 1977, the congregation of Kilmakee at Seymour Hill, a large housing estate on the outskirts of South Belfast, invited me to be their minister. In Northern Ireland terms, it was 99.9 per cent Protestant, loyalist, working class, with all the difficulties and problems one would encounter in any such area. Add to that the paramilitary activity engendered by the Troubles, and it certainly was a challenging place to be. There I ministered for nearly fourteen years, and while at times it was very hard, I counted it a real privilege to be there. I had a deep regard for those among whom I lived and worked. We were a community-based church and I found among the membership a body of people really in earnest about being relevant and alive in their area. In those early days I had a vision for the congregation, and some time later I decided to write it down. It was this: 'A place where first and foremost people would know, beyond the shadow of a doubt, that Jesus Christ is alive today and all-powerful. A church over which could be written the words we find at the end of Mark's Gospel, "And the Lord worked with them and proved that their preaching was true by the miracles that were performed". A congregation filled and motivated by a passion for God and a resulting compassion for other people. A church to which people, the lost ones, the hurting ones, the doubting ones, the searching ones, would flock, not because of any one individual but because they sensed that here, in this place and amongst these people, God lives and loves and reigns. A people who'd learned that prayer and praise were central to their living, and who knew that they couldn't take another breath unless God gave them power. A people who knew that the cross that Jesus would lay on them at this time and in this place was the burden of a torn, divided land, with all its ugly, gaping wounds, and who were willing to take up that cross and follow Him in His ministry of reconciliation'.

Well, it didn't happen, but I do believe we began to see the first fruits, and out of that ministry and those years where I feel I experienced and learned so much, probably much more than I gave, Restoration Ministries was born. The decision to leave parish ministry to work full time in Restoration Ministries has been, to date, the most major crossroads in my life. When I first became aware of the nudge within me, I tried to ignore it. It had cost me so much to 'get in' that I didn't really want to hear the call to step out, to go further. I believed that this was my 'edge of cultivation'. Also, if people had found it difficult to understand or accept ordained women, how were they ever going to understand and accept this? Besides, I was happy in Seymour Hill. I had felt that I would spend the rest of my ministry there among people I had grown to know and love. Life was not easy, but it was certainly never dull, and together we had seen many doors open, people moving from second-hand religion to living faith, and throughout the worst of the Troubles, a congregation that, by and large, was willing to reach out across the denominational divide.

During those years a ministry of prayer for healing had been emerging, especially in the area of inner healing and encouragement along the road towards the wholeness that God has had in mind for each of us from the very beginning. Early on in my time in the parish, I came across a statement that for me became a key, opening a door into a world where so much became possible. I don't know who said it first, but I began to see in my own life and then in the lives of many others, from our local congregation and much farther afield, the fruits of appropriating such a truth. It was simply this:

'God will do anything you cannot do in order that you may live. He will do nothing that you can do in order that you may grow.' People began to experience new freedom in their lives, and also began to grow and stretch and believe in something more.

Alongside this movement and, I believe, an integral part of it, was the ministry of reconciliation. There were an increasing number of cross-community ventures. Because it seemed that there were not only great divisions and lack of understanding locally, but also between North and South, gradually over the years we built up a relationship with the Carmelite Community at Gort Muire in South Dublin. Initially Gort Muire had been a refuge for me in those early years of ministry, but gradually, in ones and twos, more relationships were established and nurtured by small groups going to visit with them, and they with us. For me, this was a little sign of what was possible and what God desired for His Church.

About a year before I left parish ministry, I was able to take my Kirk Session (the Elders of the Church) to stay for a weekend with the Carmelite Fathers and Brothers in Gort Muire. One of my Elders was a member of the Orange Order. I didn't think he would come with us, but to my surprise and delight, he decided to join us. It was a memorable weekend in so many ways. But the event that lingers still so vividly in mind and heart was when I took all of our party to visit some enclosed Carmelite Sisters who lived nearby and who were dear friends of mine. We entered the parlour and sat down. The room was divided in two by a grille. After a few minutes the Sisters came in and sat on the other side. We greeted each other through the grille. They shared with us what it was like to live in an enclosed community, we told them who Presbyterian Elders were and what they did, and then we had a short act of worship together. While we were singing I chanced to look around the room, and saw several of our menfolk moved to tears. After the more formal proceedings, there was time to relax over a cup of tea, and people began to converse to and fro through the grille. At one point I happened to glance down to the other end of the room, and there, with his nose pressed tight against the wire and his tongue going twenty to the dozen, was my Orangeman. On the other side was one of the Sisters, similarly employed! It turned out that both of them had been born in Derry. Other barriers were forgotten in the remembrance of the one beloved birthplace. I prayed a silent prayer of gratitude as I witnessed this little miracle of reconciliation. Whatever way their journey has led these two individuals since then, that encounter was, I believe, an eternity moment for them, and life can never be the same.

CHAPTER FOUR

MOVING ON

Before I built a wall I'd ask to know
What I was walling in or walling out,
And to whom I was like to give offense.
Something there is that doesn't love a wall.

— Robert Frost, 'Mending Wall'[1]

Restoration Ministries takes its name from the Twenty-third Psalm 'He restores my soul'. The work was born out of a parish situation in which I worked in South Belfast, and was formalised into a charity in 1988 in order to cope with the increasing demand for its services. It is a Christian organisation seeking the healing and renewal of those involved in caring for and serving a divided and hurt society, in this way promoting peace and reconciliation. In 1991 I left the parish and began to work full-time in this new ministry. The congregation decided to sell the manse where I had lived for nearly fourteen years; it was an old house and needed some major refurbishment. We managed to get a bank loan, bought the property, and so Restoration Ministries now had a permanent base from which to work. Situated in Dunmurry, in the South Belfast area, it has easy access to both motorways and, therefore, to all parts of Ireland. A couple of years later the house was refurbished and an extension added that now facilitates our various gatherings, as well as being a safe meeting place for others on an ad hoc basis.

---

1. Frost, *Complete Poems of Robert Frost* (New York: Holt, Reinhart and Winston, 1949), p. 48.

Our calling in this organisation is to healing and reconciliation in the Irish context and beyond to those who have been in any way diminished or trapped or victimised in their own personal lives or through their communal history. One of our chief target groups is those who have been seeking to serve and give and care throughout thirty years of violence, and are now weary and spent.

We operate on a cross-community basis, and are non-denominational. Our trustees are drawn from major Christian Churches in Ireland. Apart from myself and a part-time administrator, we operate with volunteers, again drawn from all sections of the community. We are not funded by any Church or any Government agency; our journey has been and continues to be a journey of faith. Again and again we have proved the faithfulness of God through the generosity of people, enabling us to do and to be what we feel called to do and to be. A support organisation, Friends of Restoration Ministries, has over six hundred members who come from both parts of Ireland and beyond. They support us prayerfully and, where they can, financially. They receive regular newsletters and details of events.

We are a very small organisation. All we can hope to be is a little icon or sign to encourage others to do the same. In all humility, we feel called to be restorers, seeking to revitalise and renew people in the community and Church. We try to do this in several ways. A very important aspect is to provide, through our centre, a 'safe place' for people to tell their story and to be heard. Another is to help people (through courses, seminars and group work) to recognise and deal with areas of loss created by the Troubles, and also to celebrate growth and stretching. We promote the work, not in order to become a big organisation, but rather to seek to get the message across that everyone can be a restorer, everyone is needed, everyone has a part to play. So we go out into all sections of the community, both North and South, speaking, listening, pointing to windows of hope. In and through all of this we feel called, in whatever opportunities present themselves, to push out further the frontiers of what it means to have our roots go deep into a Christian culture, rather than one that is exclusively either Protestant or Catholic.

I love those words, 'Something there is that doesn't love a wall'. For me, that something is the Person of the Holy Spirit who continually creates the ground-swell, sending us out across all human barriers to discover the oneness that is ours in Christ. I'm not talking about the work of hunters, those who would ride roughshod into our lives and communities and break down a wall by force, who come perhaps out of rebellion or anger against their own traditions, and are like yelping dogs. I mean, rather, the gaps, the opportunities created by the Spirit where two can pass abreast. There are many such opportunities at this period in our history. But, in our human nature and because of all the baggage we carry with us, it is safer to keep the wall. Repeatedly in Ireland we've set the wall between us once again. One of the boulders is what could perhaps be called a bondage to the land; this thing that pulls us back, that makes us, when we leave this island for foreign shores, no longer strangers to each other, but Irish, and that roots us in this small bit of earth. When we are here, however, it twists and distorts, menaces and overshadows who we are and what we do.

In Brian Friel's play about Columba, he focuses his drama on the latter years of the saint on Iona. Columba has been in voluntary exile on Iona for years. He has done much for God, but still within him is this fighting spirit, the old ancestral lust for battle, the war cry of the O'Neills ringing in his veins, the pull of his kinsfolk and, above all, his love for Ireland. One day a messenger arrives, as has been the pattern over the years, asking him to come back to settle yet another clan dispute, and the old struggle within rears its head yet again, culminating in this final outburst from Columba: 'Get out of my life! Go back to those damned mountains and seductive hills that have robbed me of my Christ! You soaked my sweat! You sucked my blood! You stole my manhood, my best years! What more do you demand of me, damned Ireland? My soul? My immortal soul? Damned, damned, damned Ireland! Soft, green Ireland – beautiful, green Ireland.'[2]

It is significant that Friel entitles his drama 'The Enemy Within'. During recent years in Ireland there has been much to soak our sweat, to suck our blood, to steal our best years and to seek to rob us of our Christ. What hinders us more than any other factor is the enemy within, the self with its inherited bondage, its ancestral chains, as well as its own weakness and frailty.

Another boulder is a communal unforgiveness, stemming from such terrible events as the Great Famine in the 1840s. It has been said that the North will never understand the South until they come to see that the Irish have never forgiven the British for the famine; famine with its resulting land clearances, death, and emigration, seared into the communal memory. What someone has called the 'accusing ghost of black '47' has never been laid to rest, and will not be laid to rest until we invite God by His Holy Spirit into the heart of that particular darkness, claiming His grace and power to forgive so great a sin. Only then will the living stream of new life flow through the years, raising up a new generation of Irish women and men who are no longer imprisoned by hatred, bitterness and melancholy. For there is also a communal melancholy, a stronghold of sorrow, leading to mourning, self-pity, sadness and death, even a martyr complex, which has compulsively driven so many throughout the centuries and even today, to die for a change in Ireland rather than to live. And all

---

2. Brian Friel, *The Enemy Within* (Dublin: The Gallery Press, 1979), p. 70.

of that sadness and madness is accompanied by the sometimes unnatural hold of a particular type of music that stirs up at a gut level the drumbeat of nationalism or loyalism or some other 'ism', which need not be censured so long as it is not the controlling force in our lives as Christians, though I suspect that at times it is.

And if we dwell on the past in terms of our history, culture and tradition, how much more do we do so in terms of our faith. For so many people in this land, religion is also handed down. We wave flags and beat drums for the God of our Fathers, but if we were to ask the sons and daughters who He is, how many would know? The 'faith', tested and proved by those who have gone before us, is often only theory or myth to the present generation. It seems to me that a spirit of religion, militating against active, believing faith, is another boulder in the wall. It produces a hardness, a legalism, a bigotry and a prejudice that controls and directs lives, rather than the Spirit of the living God.

These, and many other boulders, are the things that separate us, that imprison us. We may make sorties out to greater openness and freedom, but when crises hit, the tentacles of this octopus will pull us back to our particular ghetto or prison cell within.

We put so much effort into keeping the wall there. To the outside world it seems like just another game. For, so often, the wall is not necessary; we do not need the barricades. There is nothing of which we need be afraid. And yet we are so conditioned. We can make the drumbeat in the gut coming down through the centuries so real and so rational when we hear quoted words such as 'Good fences make good neighbours'. And it is with a huge sense of relief that we readily concur, 'Yes, it's only sensible and right'.

Part of choosing this road of reconciliation, of pushing out the frontiers, is to dare to ask the question clearly, standing our ground: 'Why? Why do good fences make good neighbours? Why do we need to have the wall? What are we walling in or walling out?' And while it may offend some, while they may even become very angry at the slightest crossing of the line, to whom are we likely to give offence by walling each other out? None other than Jesus Himself who continually, in His earthly ministry, crossed the line, and who calls us again and again to love one another, to be one so that the world may believe; Jesus, who does not love a wall, who by His own body has broken it down between us.

What is it, that ancient force as strong or stronger today than hundreds of years ago, that keeps so many immobile, an irresistible force that will not budge, that will not yield or surrender? It is as if we too are, to quote Frost again, like 'some old stone savage armed', moving in darkness, which is not the darkness of woods or the shade of trees, but the darkness of a greater force, handed down – a strong conditioning or imprisoning throughout the years. We need to name it, to say it for ourselves. Instead, we will not let go of our fathers' sayings, with all the swirling emotion behind them. We find a respectable way of keeping the wall and congratulate ourselves on having exercised wisdom and caution. 'Good fences make good neighbours.' Repeatedly, Scripture contradicts this, calling us to become people of hospitality for each other, to risk allowing others in, to disarm ourselves, to find the gaps where two can pass abreast. 'Something there is that does not love a wall.'

While I have been writing this chapter, on nearly every occasion when I have been trying to get my thoughts into some order and onto paper, there has been a phone call, or someone calling at the door, or unexpected guests coming to stay. For several days I could not understand why there were so many interruptions, when there were time schedules to meet that were really important. There was even a point when I began to panic that it would never come to fruition. And then, all of a sudden, a light went on inside me. I realised what God had been wanting me to recognise all along, namely that it was much more important to 'do it' than to write or talk about it, that these were no interruptions, but rather the very stuff of what we are about as people of welcome. What matters is that, over these weeks, many people have crossed the threshold of Restoration House and even the threshold of our hearts, and, please God, have found there welcome and acceptance. And we? Well, we have encountered and entertained angels unawares.

It takes some time to become the sort of place or community where, when people come, they just know they will be welcome, where they even expect it. It's a privilege, but it's also costly. I have a friend who lives just up the road from me at Restoration House. He is a regular caller at this house but I never know when he's coming. He arrives and just assumes that I'll be glad to see him. That expectation in him must have come from something in the atmosphere of the place, or in my attitude or reaction to him, because even if there are times when I wish him anywhere but here, he is so assured of his welcome that he doesn't notice my less-than-effusive response. You see, he is so handsome and he has such a heart-melting way of putting his head on one side and looking at me with his big eyes, that immediately I'm caught, I'm his slave. He just comes to the front door, and waits. After we have had some conversation, and he has had refreshment and feels he has graced me with his company long enough, he walks off. A moment later, however, he pushes his luck too far and tries the same tactic at the back door, with similar assurance. And, yes, of course I give in! His name is Prince. Now, I don't really like dogs, I'm actually a little afraid of them. I need to know them for quite some time before I begin to trust them even a tiny bit. But, somehow, both of us seemed to throw caution to the wind and risk this friendship. There has been a mutual welcome, and both have been blessed – Prince with biscuits, and I with a warm sort of feeling that dog and I can be friends!

It's a simple example that can tap very deeply into other scenarios within ourselves. Hospitality, welcoming the stranger in our midst (the stranger often meaning the one who is different, marginalised, outcast, even the enemy), is at the core of the Gospel. Jesus said, 'Love your enemies. Pray for those who persecute you. If you are kind only to your friends how are you different from anyone else? Even pagans do that' (Mt 5:44, 47). And yet, we're afraid. Fear of difference and fear of the unknown are the enemies of welcome. They cause separation and division. We find it easier to label 'them', 'the other', the 'outsider', not primarily thinking of them as fellow human beings, sisters and brothers. We do build walls, but the wonderful and scary thing is that Jesus keeps knocking them down, and, if we have the slightest chink of openness, entertaining angels becomes not a far-fetched notion, but distinctly within the bounds of 'God-possibility'. True hospitality does not pick and choose; it is all-inclusive and shows a God-embrace for the one who knocks on our door.

In some small measure in Restoration Ministries we seek to be agents or facilitators of such hospitality in various ways – by offering a prayer ministry on an individual and confidential basis, by organising seminars and workshops, by providing a haven for those in need of space, quiet and rest for a few days, and by encouraging, in every way we can, the building of relationships, friendships and trust between people from all traditions.

I remember during the time of the first ceasefire paying a return visit after some years to my dear friends, the Benedictine Sisters at Kylemore Abbey in Connemara. During that stay I asked them if some of them would consider coming to visit us in the North. After some understandable hesitation they agreed. It was a memorable day when, on their autumn mid-term break, three of the Sisters drove into our carpark at Restoration House. None of them had been North before. The weekend was packed full of fun and laughter, and of serious moments of encounter. On the Sunday evening, we threw an open-house, when many people from all sections of the wider community came. This, like all other open-house times here, had two purposes: firstly, that our visitors could meet local people, and secondly, and most importantly, that local people could meet each other in a safe place such as this. The following day there was a tour of Belfast, followed by a visit from Cardinal Daly. The Sisters' visit coincided with a monthly meeting to which all are welcome at Restoration House. Our theme for that particular year was 'What it means to be a citizen of heaven in the present ceasefire situation'. I asked them if they would be our speakers, and if they would be honest about their view of history, what they thought about the North, and about England. Their immediate reaction was, 'Oh, but we wouldn't want to hurt or offend anybody', to which my only reply could be, 'But if we're ever going to move forward in Ireland to something better, then we've got to be honest with each other.' So, they did it, very sensitively, and then led us in a beautiful reflection on peace. At the end of the evening one of the Sisters came and flung her arms around me. 'I feel as if, over this weekend, I have shed the burden of six hundred years of history', she said, 'and I never again will think about the North the way I have.' And I remember praying silently, 'Lord, if nothing else happens in this house all year, it is enough. Thank you.'

The next morning the Sisters started for home. On arrival they gave an account of their visit to the rest of their community. When they had finished, the entire community rose and went to their chapel where they lit a candle and prayed for us in Restoration Ministries and for peace in Northern Ireland. They have been doing so ever since.

For me, the good news is that we already belong together in the embrace of God's perfect love. It's just that many haven't discovered it yet. Because they haven't, then those who have begun to see it are called to the ministry of reconciliation, of hospitality, of welcoming the stranger, so that more and more people may reach a similar discovery, and rejoice.

And the road we're asked to travel is a costly one. One of the most pointed stories Jesus told about this sort of journey, this sort of hospitality, was the story of the Good Samaritan. I think of the Jericho to Jerusalem road as the reconciliation road. I deliberately say Jericho to Jerusalem because for those who seek to be bearers of hospitality, healers, peacemakers, the way will certainly lead to Jerusalem, to the place of crucifixion. It's the road of danger, of misunderstanding. Along its route are robbers and powers of darkness, whose aim is to destroy or render ineffective those who travel it. There are those who pay lip-service to it because that is what is expected of them in these days, but like the priest and the Levite, when danger threatens or when risk is called for, they hurry by, not wanting to get involved. On this road, there is an inn, a place of refuge, a place of safety. Only a fool would build an inn on such a road! Maybe he had no other option, or maybe he felt compelled or called; whatever the reason, the innkeeper is there, ready to offer hospitality to any lonely or weary stranger who chooses or has to travel this particular road, for the role of the innkeeper as well as that of the Samaritan could be our vocation. When the Samaritan brought the wounded man to the inn, he said to the innkeeper, 'Take care of him, and if you spend more, I will pay you when I come.' Maybe the question for each one of us, in these precious, fragile days, is 'What does it mean to spend more? What does it mean for me to spend more in terms of peace, unity and reconciliation, in the building of bridges, in being open and vulnerable?' You can imagine, as the days pass, the innkeeper going to the door of his inn, scanning the horizon to see whether he is coming. And in the meantime he and his guest bring gifts to each other, living community together, strangers becoming friends – entertaining angels.

To be people of hospitality for each other is at the heart of our calling as Christians; to live it out, to allow ourselves to spend more, to be open-hearted and forgiving as we wait for the God who has promised to restore fully when He comes back.

CHAPTER FIVE

THE WAY HOME

Give me your hand,
Perhaps we still have a long way to go.
It's snowing, it's snowing.
Winter is a hard thing in a strange country.

— Herman Hesse, 'Evil Time'[1]

I remember years ago, when I was learning to swim, I was quite nervous and fearful, afraid I would sink, go under, drown. It was all very well to paddle, even to let the water come up to my knees, but actually to risk taking my feet off the bottom and trust that the water would hold me up, without too much effort on my part, was another matter. Now I see that I just needed to co-operate and it would happen. I always needed to be sure that, if I let go of the edge of the pool, it was within easy reach again. Or, if I was in the sea, I needed the assurance of being able to touch the sandy floor with at least my big toe! Even now I have to admit that, if I'm swimming and find myself suddenly out of my depth, I could easily panic, and I hasten to reach a place where I can feel safer and more in control.

I would never have learnt to swim if I hadn't taken both feet off the bottom and let go of the edge. So, too, a boat will never go out deeper, never reach the ocean, see other horizons, or head for another shore, if it remains in its mooring, if it doesn't weigh anchor.

There is always a tension in life between what is felt to be the safe

---

1. Herman Hesse, *Poems* (London: Jonathan Cape Ltd, 1971), p. 41.

place, the place that is home, and the unfamiliar, uncharted territory. Nowhere is this more evident than in the whole area of reconciliation, of building or restoring relationships between ourselves and God, or within our own inner beings, or between ourselves and other people. There is that in me which strives to be in control, to know beforehand exactly what is happening, to protect myself, and to remain in familiar surroundings, even if at times they are cramped, uncomfortable, boring or unproductive. I cling onto the edge for all I'm worth. I will not let go. But then there comes the gentle whisper that keeps insisting that there is something more, a fullness of life of which I've only caught a glimpse and, in order to find it, I must strike out from the shore. I cannot ask others to go this way if I am not prepared to travel that way myself. Once again, the outer reflects the inner.

I have been so grateful for friends on the journey. That sense of their accompanying presence is so warming and encouraging. It wraps me around, giving me an assurance of companionship, of belonging, a conviction that all will be well, that although there may be darkness, tragedies, disasters along the way, the destination is certain and I do not travel alone.

But there are also times when it seems as if none of this is present, that I am journeying totally on my own, that there is no light shining for me, no hand to hold. There are times when I am weary and spent, and I cannot see the way ahead. This is, I believe, the lot of all pilgrims at certain stages, when we somehow find ourselves in a strange country, a place of exile, where it seems like winter, with little or no sign of life. It is at times such as these that we are confronted most starkly with the inner journey of reconciliation, the toughest travelling we will ever do. Our attitudes and reactions almost subconsciously draw their life from those parts of us we would rather were not there, the bits we do not like. At the same time, we know that the fundamental call to the Christian is to live as one whose whole being reflects the upside-down attitudes of the Kingdom, the 'be-attitudes', the overriding characteristic of which is joy.

Whenever I think of personal freedom, of travelling further, of wholeness, there is a particular image that comes to mind. It epitomises for me the return of the exile within, the inner reconciliation journey. It is a dancing spirit.

I remember very clearly, though for a great part of my life I chose not to remember, the first dance I ever went to. I was seventeen years old, and it was our school formal. There was great excitement. Many of the girls were going with partners. I was going on my own, and I was apprehensive, even scared. But I also desperately wanted to go. Somehow I hoped, wished, prayed that all the things that would act as a barrier – the worry as to whether anyone would notice me and ask me to dance; anxiety about how I looked; hesitancy about entering a room full of people who, it seemed to me, were confident and assured; self-consciousness; fear of not getting it right; the desire to be fully a part of that happy bunch – would fade into insignificance, and that the dancing spirit that was around even then would break free and, literally, have a ball!

Well, I have to say that the dancing spirit remained as a caged bird! All my worst scenarios took place. And even when one of my classmates took pity on me and asked her escort to dance with me (my only dance of the evening), I was so naive that I did not know that there were three dances to a set, so when we had danced one, I thanked him and moved away! The excruciating shame and embarrassment I felt when I discovered my 'mistake' were overwhelming. It has taken many years to reach the point of recognising that all of these feelings and reactions were part of an inner woundedness that, for different reasons and in varying degrees, are the lot of every person. I have also realised that we are called, not to push these things away, but rather to restore hospitality to those parts of ourselves that we have for so long kept in exile. Hidden in the shadows are things like loneliness, anger, rejection, fear, jealousy, caution, mistrust. But also, locked away with them, often buried underneath them, are so much creativity and unexpressed potential, which will never come to light unless we are willing to let the exile return, and to be able to see and name and risk finally putting some of these things to rest or else to allow other things to have life, because we have come home to ourselves.

It's only within very recent times that I chose to go to dancing classes, and I really enjoyed them, restoring the years that the locusts had eaten! It was a little outward sign that, by a long and often tortuous road, the outer is beginning to reflect the inner, and the inner the outer.

How can I let the dance begin? There is a sense in which mine is no unique condition. We have all inherited things that cause part of us to be exiled. We have all been wounded in our early lives. These, along with our own ready ability to walk into areas of imprisonment due to our rebellion, mean that there's a big act of bringing back or redemption to be done in each one of us. There are always more bits of me to be redeemed and brought home. But the journey is possible, gloriously so, because of Jesus our Redeemer. Whoever we are, wherever we come from, this inner work, this acknowledgement of who we are in entirety, this creation of community within is vital and necessary. There is great joy in the gift of discovering that what we once considered our worst feature, our weakest 'member', is the one that, once it's 'home', can be our greatest strength. It is an act of courage and faith to go on this journey back to the essence of who we are, in order that we might be an integral part of God's choreography in the dance to which we are all invited.

All of us are handicapped, wounded, broken, and many of us are experts at hiding it. The reasons why we don't show our shadow side stem from fear — fear of being rejected if 'they' really knew us, or fear of being taken over or trapped. Yet, subconsciously, that is what we are doing to ourselves. We are rejecting those parts, exiling them rather than entering into dialogue with them. In order to be in control, the so-called adult takes over and locks them away. This is an effective enough strategy in the short term, but sooner or later the cry of the exile is going to be heard, through physical illness, emotional trauma, or something.

Deep within us there is often an aching loneliness stemming from this sense of exile; a deep loneliness usually because of the wounds of long ago. How do we begin to hear the voice that urges us to come back home, to come to ourselves? It's a call for us to go further, to go deeper with Jesus, that we might become all that He intends. Such a call is costly, but will prove so worthwhile in the end. It's a call to awaken, to dare to let those parts of our beings that have been anaesthetised for so many long years to come around. And we awaken to joy and sorrow, to ecstasy and pain, for that is life, real life.

I remember once, when I was sixteen years old, falling off my bicycle on my way to school. I broke my leg very badly and tore all the ligaments. I was in plaster and on crutches for four months. When the plaster finally came off, the damaged leg was about one third the width of the other one. The muscles hadn't been used for so long that they had wasted and become almost useless. Doing exercises to bring them back to life, learning to walk again, was excruciatingly painful, more painful than the initial injury. And yet, the pain was a sign of life returning rather than of disease or decay. So, too, with our inner life as we go deeper, as we risk searching for the dead parts, allowing the Spirit to blow the breath of life into these exiled areas, there will be pain, but also abundant life.

This call to truly live, to travel further, involves a decision to go searching for the exiled part of us. It is so important that we first experience God's welcome of us, for without it, we would not have the courage to go on such a journey. It will take us deeper. But once we have encountered, even a little, the embrace of Jesus, then there comes a point where we know that it is really God Himself who is leading us on this journey, and in the going we discover that it becomes, in a strange way, the place of healing. While it is true that such a journey is ultimately made on our own with God, there are times when we need someone to give us their hand, because perhaps we still have a long way to go. In Restoration Ministries we seek, among other things, to be that hand to those who courageously choose to travel such a way, to listen, to pray, simply to be there for them when the road is too long, or the night too lonely.

It's a journey of faith, a call to risk touching a part of our inner selves that we had avoided coming into contact with, and to discover, in the darkness, a treasure. It's a call to give up wishing or pretending that we're perfect, while inwardly knowing that it's not true, and to realise that being who we are is all that is important.

For many of us it is the challenge to be present to the wounded child within. It is the wounded child who is in the place of exile, who has perhaps long since given up all hope of being welcomed back home, and yet, without whom, we will not reach home.

I have always loved the story of Ruth and Naomi in the Old Testament. I have felt that it is somehow a little picture of my own journey, or perhaps that of any human being who is travelling through life and is seeking to be at home with themselves, who is wanting to join the dance. It is as if within me dwell Naomi the adult and Ruth the child, although for a long time I was not so aware of Ruth. For years, as Naomi, I have been hungry for more wholeness, for more truth, for more growth, and also hungry for 'home' in a deep way. I've gone to strange and unfamiliar places, my particular Moab, searching, like Naomi. And through it all, God has been present. He has always been there. Then, through various happenings, as life has unfolded, I have become aware of Ruth, the child. I, as Naomi, want to go home, to be 'at home' with myself and with God. So I have been searching and striving, and sometimes, like Naomi, I have felt my name was Mara, meaning bitter. But then I imagine that my inner child, Ruth, is saying to me, 'You'll not really reach that sense of at-homeness without me'. She is saying, 'Don't ask me to leave you and turn back. I will go wherever you go and live wherever you live. Your people will be my people and your God will be my God' (Ruth 1:16). And I know that it is all of me that needs to come to Bethlehem, to that place where it seems as if I'm totally empty, but is, in reality, the place of new life, of bread for the world, of hope. When that happens, when, in that sense, I come to myself, it is harvest time, and there will be fruit in my life. It is the return of the exile, Naomi and Ruth together, a coming together within, and then there is peace; adult and unacknowledged or trapped inner child, gift to one another, reconciled in order that Jesus may be given to the world.

There is always something more to be discovered. Maybe what I'm learning is that, no matter what stage of life we're at, the challenge is to dare to listen for the unfamiliar tune, and to sing our song, to risk moving with a rhythm that may at first seem strange, and to let our spirit dance, so that the world may believe in a God who dances, and who continually and lovingly calls the exiles to return.

CHAPTER SIX

FOOD FOR THE JOURNEY

The woods are lovely, dark and deep
But I have promises to keep.
And miles to go before I sleep
And miles to go before I sleep.
— Robert Frost
'Stopping By Woods On a Snowy Evening'[1]

In a quiet corner of Restoration House is a little prayer room, a place of presence and peace for any weary pilgrim who needs a resting place. In the busiest hub of the same house, the kitchen, everything comes to a halt each day at noon as we gather to pray for peace. At the same time we open the precious book in which are written all the names of the people whom we have covenanted to remember. It is a real encouragement to us that many others throughout Ireland and beyond join us at this time. On a regular basis those who have been wounded, or have come to a stumbling block on their journey, make their way to another room where, accompanied by members of our prayer ministry team, they are enabled to leave some of their burdens down and travel on with a lighter step. Every evening, before he goes home, Arthur, our longtime volunteer, walks around the outside of the house, anointing the doors and gateposts, praying protection for place and people. Recently, in preparation for the Millennium, we were joined by friends of Restoration Ministries from various parts of the world in a round-the-clock four days of prayer for fresh vision and courage, as

1. Frost, *Complete Poems of Robert Frost*, p. 275.

well as for other places of difficulty and brokenness around the globe. So, prayer is central to our life, providing us with food for the journey. Without that nurturing, we could not take another step.

It seems to me that in terms of our history in the island of Ireland, we are at the crucial point, perhaps just beginning to emerge from 'the darkest evening of the year'. Every step we take, or decide not to take, has an effect. All sorts of promises beckon us forward, and all sorts of demons drive us back. The road can be hard, and the years of conflict have produced great weariness. Maybe the most important lesson we have to learn is that we need to stop, to watch, to listen, to rest in Jesus so that we have the strength and the resources to be once again on our way, to keep the promises. Yes, it is time, as never before, to put our lives where our words have been, to move very deliberately with wisdom, beyond caution, to encourage each other (that is, to gift one another with courage). But in order to do that, and because we have miles to go before we sleep, we need to take the time to watch, to listen, 'between the woods and frozen lake' – in the midst of all that is dark and hard and unyielding, to rest in Him and to let Him rest in us. Otherwise the journey will be too much. How can I travel such a road, unless I have the security of knowing that I am the beloved of Jesus? For me, this is the important part of the whole process. If I don't do this, if I do not have this assurance, then not very far down the line I am going to crumple. It is a Jerusalem road, and as we seek to walk it faithfully, the Rubicon behind us, it will be the way that Jesus walked. What I'm really talking about here is prayer, prayer as a love relationship with Jesus that then leads to prayer-motivated action.

'Lord, teach us to pray' was the request, maybe even the cry from the heart, of the disciples of Jesus long ago. That cry reverberates down through the centuries, and finds more than a passing echo in many hearts. In fact, at times it can become almost a deafening scream, 'Lord, teach us to pray. Lord, show us how.' I sometimes think, 'If those disciples who were living with Jesus, sharing His life in every respect, had to ask that question, what hope have I?' Most of us, when it boils down to it, have difficulty with prayer. We don't know what we should be doing. 'There must be something more', the tiny voice whispers, or sometimes shouts, inside of us, yet we rarely speak it out because of what other people might think of us – 'other people' in church who have always thought of us as great believers or great people of prayer.

Someone once said to my father, 'I'm a great believer in prayer.' He replied, 'Well – I'm not, I'm not! I'm a great believer in Jesus.' He wasn't saying he didn't believe in praying, but he was trying to point the person beyond to what prayer is all about, which is that love relationship with God as we know Him in Jesus.

'Lord, teach us to pray, Lord, show us how' is really coming from the ache within every human being, whether they recognise it or not, for more of God. It points to the fact, I believe, that in each person there is a God-shaped 'hole' that only God can fill. That 'hole' will never be fully satisfied this side of death, for there's always more. That's part of what makes the Christian life so exciting. For just as faith is a journey, so also is prayer – a journey into relationship.

I went to Queen's University when I was just seventeen years old. I was very shy and, having been at an all-girls' school, the world of university took a little getting used to. While I had been brought up in a Christian home by parents who were faithful prayer partners, and a minister's family at that (with all the extra expectations placed upon one in those days by the immediate external community of the Church), I never felt at liberty to ask the question 'Will you teach me how to pray?', that is, not to 'say' my prayers, but to pray. This was partly because I felt that 'they' thought I should know already, and partly because I didn't want to let anyone down. In my first term at

Queen's, I went to a Student Christian Movement conference, at which there was a well-known speaker from another country. I remember summoning up all my courage and asking to see him on my own, to put to him this same question which by then was coming from the very gut of my being, 'Teach me to pray; can you tell me how?' When, instead of answering my request, he handed me a book to read, my sense of disappointment was overwhelming. It was years later before I felt I could ask anyone again. Now, with the wisdom of the years and the compassion of hindsight, I can see that the poor man himself, maybe, had the same ache or cry deep within his being, so that he could not answer me; he perhaps did not know either.

There have probably been more books written on prayer than on any other subject in the world, many of them claiming to be an authority. I find that the danger in reading too may books is that it can serve as an escape from actually doing it, actually praying. The only 'authority' I know is Jesus Himself, and prayer is, at its most basic and highest, an entering into and growing in that loving friendship with Him. It seems to me that what we bring to corporate prayer, praying together, stems from the quality of what we experience on our own before Him. If I am merely 'saying' my prayers as distinct from praying, if I am merely repeating by rote what I have always done, taking no time to be in His presence, to listen, to grow in relationship, if my praying is squeezed into a few minutes when all the 'important' issues of the day have been dealt with, then I cannot wonder that my prayer life is dull and devoid of expectancy, or that what I experience when I come together with others is often something that has little life – just words.

For me, a key lies in being willing to open myself up to the very basic but profound question, 'Do you know that you are loved, and special? Do you know that Jesus loves you; that just as you are right now, with all the bits that He can see and others can't, you are accepted, cherished, beautiful in His sight?' If I don't, and most of us don't, then there's a big job to do. We can feel so guilty, so unlovable: we imagine we'd be rejected if others saw us as we really are. We're afraid of intimacy, afraid of the darkness within ourselves, afraid even of the word 'love'. We can even be fearful of Jesus, seeking to keep Him at a distance, referring to Him by what we feel is the more remote title of God. So we put the lid on, and rush around trying all sorts of remedies to anaesthetise the pain, one of the chief remedies being busyness. We never dare to take the time just to be without words in His presence, to let Him draw close and begin to touch, ever so gently, the sore points within – the low self-worth, the inadequacy, the fear, the woundedness, so that we begin to know what it is to be loved and held by God, not in our superficial perfection, but in all our brokenness and littleness, a God who knows, and who has let Himself become little and broken for us.

To keep company with Jesus, to relax into the reality of being loved by God, is prayer, so that we then become image-bearers of Him. For me, hospitality or welcome is so much part of prayer – not only Jesus welcoming me as I seek to be with Him, but me welcoming Him into a place that is intimate and deep. There I begin to relax in knowing that, while there is still an awful lot of spring-cleaning to be done in this 'home' that is me, and maybe some renovation or restoration work as well, right at this moment, just as I am, He is glad to be here, and my heart must respond in gladness. It's out of that security of welcome, of being loved, that I can truly enter into worship – praise, adoration, confession, repentance. To be confronted by my sin and by my shadow side without that security leads to self-condemnation, extra guilt, or else a pretending that that side of me does not exist, that all I have to do is to strive even harder to be perfect. If I do that I fall into the trap of self-atonement and wear myself out. Then I wonder why everything is so wearying, so boring, so lifeless. I become dominated by what others think, and much that is worthwhile is silenced.

Over the last few years in Ireland, people, I believe, have been much more tuned into the necessity and the importance of prayer. This may have been partly because many had reached a point of weariness and a real desperation for peace, and partly because it seemed as if everything else had been tried and it was 'down to God now!' Whatever the reason, people have been praying as never before, prepared to go deeper, willing this time to trust that Jesus is their only hope for any lasting peace. And out of the crucible of so many shattered hopes and broken dreams, of so much bitterness and unforgiveness, of long years of mistrust, suspicion and prejudice, something is being forged that, in spite of delays and even mighty stumbling blocks, we trust and pray, heralds the dawn of a new era for a land that for far too long has known deep divisions and hatreds. Those who bear the Name of Jesus, from whatever tradition they come, know that the real Peace Agreement, the one that makes every other peace agreement possible, was already signed two thousand years ago, on that first Good Friday. It was the willing signature of Jesus to the peace plan of God that had been in His heart from before the foundation of the world, Jesus signing in His own blood an end to the separation between God and humankind, and to the dividing walls of hostility that we persist in building between us. Jesus has already done it! He is our peace! Maybe at last, after so many years of not seeing, some people in Ireland are beginning to understand that truth, a truth that transcends all other truths and that right now gives us to each other in the oneness that is already ours in Him.

Food for the journey comes through prayer and also through the living words of Scripture. Increasingly, I have found nurture along the way in what for me are basic guidelines for living, the Beatitudes.

It's so easy to say 'yes' to these lovely words, but when the chips are down, they're hard words, they're words of challenge, radical and uncomfortable. I suppose really I'm not ready to be poor; I would rather avoid the sorrow and the mourning: the concept of meekness or gentleness frightens me with the possibility of being trampled upon. I don't sit easily with hunger and thirst, and while it's the Christian thing to do to be merciful, sometimes hitting back can be very satisfying and perhaps justifiable. To be pure in heart might mean missing out on something I really rather enjoy: peace-loving is an easier concept than peacemaking; and to rejoice when people revile you is a bit over the top! Or is it?

Any peace process will only become a reality when attitudes change, when we allow our minds to be stretched, invaded, conquered by the Spirit of truth, the frontiers pushed out, taken over by God, and the doors of our hearts opened, the curtains drawn back, the blinds pulled up, and love, in the Person of Jesus, allowed in, in all His fullness. The Beatitudes embody the Person and the Spirit of Jesus. Given at the outset of His earthly ministry, they are the charter for all who would journey ever afterwards. And there's always more to learn. It doesn't happen all at once; we 'become'. It is a journey, often an uphill climb. We are not yet what we shall be, but as we dare to believe that there is a place beyond the end, as we seek to counter individual and community paralysis, as we choose life, as we shake ourselves awake and risk reclaiming the vision, as we recognise ourselves truly as a community of the broken, the little wounded ones and, maybe most of all, as we leave ourselves open and willing 'to make the broken place sing',[2] then, in all humility, blessed are we, and blessed is He who in the end has not left us to make this journey alone.

---

2. Kathy Galloway, *Struggles to Love* (London: SPCK, 1994), p. 14.

The whole of Good News living could, I believe, be summed up in these eight sayings of Jesus, that really paint a picture of the sort of life He wants of us, the sort of life God smiles upon, that warms His heart. These statements shatter many myths; they lead us into strange truth, an unfamiliar, upside-down kingdom, but a real one nonetheless, which we eventually find is the right way up! And in the travelling, while it may at times seem as if we are going down instead of up, down into the valley of the shadow or into the abyss of nothingness, the more we persist, the more glimpses we get of other peaks, until one day we shall stand at the top, through Him, with Him, in Him, and see clearly. Often blessedness comes in no other way but the hard way. We could settle for less; it would be tempting to go for the easy option, but that leads to nothing except stagnation. It's journeying time and there is always something more. The Beatitudes urge us forward, keep us travelling. They seem impossible, but each one of them in themselves is a journey towards the Kingdom, towards wholeness, towards life in all its fullness. As we, not as perfect individuals, but as ordinary mortals who recognise the collegiality of the feet of clay, seek to live them, then we bless each other, we bless the community in which we live and work and worship, and we bless the world.

On this journey, as well as us keeping promises, or being the agents to help fulfil God's promises, there are also promises made to us; hundreds of houses, brothers, sisters, mothers, children, friends – and persecutions as well. It's not all one or the other. On the Jerusalem road, Jesus and His followers had lots of celebration times as well. We need to set out with joy, as we go forth in peace. The whole of creation is involved in this, I believe – all that God has made, including ourselves here in Ireland, who are stumbling little pilgrims, all groaning with eager longing for what is up ahead. This island that has been held under a cloud of melancholy and doom for so long has mountains and hills just bursting to break forth into singing, and trees in every field aching to clap their hands, because up ahead is the 'possible' of God. Ireland can yet show the world something. In all its littleness, brokenness, stubbornness and division, in all its woundedness – a light to the nations, a sign of hope to a weary world, a heartbeat of peace – as it points beyond itself to the One who, at the eleventh hour, is calling it forth from death to life.

What do I want, before I sleep? I want to choose, with my feet firmly on the ground, and my eyes fixed on Jesus; I want to choose the road less travelled by. I want with my life to stand against the lie that good fences make good neighbours, to allow the stone savage in me and in others to be disarmed, to shout aloud to all those caught in fear or hatred or unforgiveness that a farther shore is reachable even from here. I want most of all, in some small way, to be, along with my sisters and brothers from every tradition, an image-bearer of Jesus in this most crucial time of our history, and in doing so to be able to sing because the dawn is coming. For the journey doesn't end with Jerusalem. As we take the road, as we find food for the journey and wine for rejoicing, we remember that we are an Easter people. Through the power of the cross and resurrection, the road we dare to take will make all the difference. And somewhere, ages and ages hence, we, or those who follow after us, will be telling this, not with a sigh, but with a Hallelujah!

In the meantime, there are promises to keep. And miles to go before we sleep.

CHAPTER SEVEN

A PLACE BEYOND THE END

Though we live in a world that thinks of ending,
That always seems about to give in,
Something that will not acknowledge conclusion
Insists that we forever begin.

– Brendan Kennelly, 'Begin'[1]

My father and I were really good friends, as well as being father and daughter. I remember very clearly, on the evening before I left for Canada, knowing I would not be home for two years, he came into the room where I was doing some last-minute packing. He stood there, with tears in his eyes, holding a piece of paper in his hand. He had written a poem for me, as his way of expressing how he felt at this goodbye. It began like this:

How can I say
Goodbye?
My whole being
reaches out
to hold you
within the security
of home,
parent love
striving with itself
to hold

---

1. Brendan Kennelly, *Selected Poems* (Dublin: Allen Figgis Ltd, 1969), p. 43.

yet let go,
possessive,
yet longing
that you become
a person
in your own right,
bound to home,
yet free
to lay hold
on life.
No longer child,
you stand
with parents
as equal
in life's journey,
leading now
where once led,
giving hope
and courage
to wearier feet.

He said he felt that he stood under the judgement of this goodbye, in the poem questioning whether he had given me the vision that would lift me to my feet again when beaten down in life's battle, that would call me from despair's dark gloom to see the light still touching the distant hills. He wondered if he had given me the faith that would hold cynicism at bay, giving no place to bitterness, but seeing life as destiny worked out before the face of God. He asked, perhaps most poignantly, if I had seen in him a little light on why people call God 'Father', and whether he had started me on that road that leads through light and shade to the uplands where we behold the Kingdom of the living God.

Any traveller needs to be prepared for many hellos and goodbyes, and new hellos along the way; to know how to let go in order to embrace the new and to move on. It's costly, it's painful, but if one has a pilgrim heart, this attitude produces growth, depth, sensitivity and so much else along the way. Jesus knew so much about hello and goodbye. He knew par excellence, and practised that welcome that allows us to go as well as come, that allows people to be truly themselves, and not to be possessed or manipulated. Some of the most moving verses in the Gospels are those where Jesus is saying goodbye to His friends: 'But now I am going away to the one who sent me, and none of you has asked me where I am going. Instead, you are very sad. But it is actually best for you that I go away, because if I don't, the Counsellor won't come. If I do go away, he will come because I will send him to you.... Oh, there is so much more I want to tell you, but you can't bear it now.... In just a little while I will be gone, and you won't see me any more. Then just a little while after that, you will see me again' (Jn 16:5-6, 12, 16).

Life is full of hellos and goodbyes, and new hellos. We discover as we go that a true hello is costly, and that letting go or goodbye is even more so. Between our first hello at birth, and the final goodbye of our death, there are many comings and goings. Some people find these difficult to cope with, so rather than be hurt, they live on the fringes of involvement, not investing too much of themselves, but underneath crying for love, for friendship, for intimacy. Others, knowing it will cost, still dare to respond to the call to be wide open, recognising that there will be agony and ecstasy, death and resurrection. When they come to the end of their days here on earth and enter that new, unknown stage of 'life', they will discover, I believe, that Eternity does not begin at some vague point after death, but has already dawned for them in all their eternity moments of their earthly journeys, when they allowed themselves to be aware, alert, fully alive – alive to others, alive to God, alive to the world about them, alive to themselves.

At the end of that summer together in Vancouver, we, as participants, had grown together as a community. On leaving, one of the team wrote a reflection, part of which went as follows:

> *To say hello is to grow, but to say goodbye is to grow the more,*
> *for it takes an effort to reach beyond oneself to another, and that*
>   *effort produces growth,*
> *but it takes much more effort to let go, to let that part of*
> *yourself that you gave to another person be really given.*
> *To say hello is of God, but to say goodbye is to commit one's love to*
>   *the care of God.*
> *…But most of all, to have said hello and goodbye to a*
> *great soul is to have come face to face with God*
> *and to know His love.*

One such great soul was Margaret Newell, dear companion on the journey for just a couple of years before her death. But in that short time she gave all of us in Restoration Ministries so much. Wherever Margaret was, there was laughter and music and encouragement. We prayed so earnestly for her healing, feeling she was leaving us too soon. We loved her; she loved us. Yet through her journeying on to the place beyond the end, we have learned to commit our love to the care of God, and to know that in the unseen crowd of witnesses there is laughter and music – and such encouragement. Goodbye really means 'God be with you'. It means *'Vaya con Dios!'* – go with God! So, we do not go alone. Nor do we leave the loved one behind alone. God is a central part of hello and goodbye.

And when the way seems heavy and hard, what can lift us to our feet again and keep us journeying? It is when we re-member, call to mind, give flesh again to those times when we've been blessed and loved and cherished, those times when we've felt in communion with another, with God and with His creation, those times when we've known a purpose, been grasped by a vision, when we were certain that we had been gifted with pilgrimage. What a privilege! And the pilgrim moves on, empowered by gratitude.

So, what is up ahead? And where are we going? In the end it is mystery. No one knows, but we believe. I have a friend who is in two minds about heaven. She can think of nothing more boring than standing in rows, singing unendingly from *Mission Praise*! If a qualification for being in heaven is singing, my father would never have made it! But I believe he is there, part of that beloved community. When he died, after a funeral service in Lisburn, his body was taken 'home' to Donegal, to Ballymore, between Creeslough and Dunfanaghy. I remember very vividly, on 30 September 1991, that when the cortège was still about five miles from its destination, the road was lined with people who had come out from the whole Dunfanaghy area to welcome one of their own back home. There was something profoundly moving and comforting about that. And once again, words from that poem he had written twenty-five years previously came flooding into my mind:

> *Goodbye*
> *for faith*
> *is not the end*
> *but the new beginning*
> *that ever lies*
> *in God's power to give.*
> *Grace covers all the past*

and opens doors into a future
brighter still,
for God goes before
and what is past
cannot hold dominion
over that which
God has planned
for you
who are far dearer
to Him than me.
You remain His child.
He is a refuge always
for you, as me
till goodbye
need no more
be said.

The day after he died, my mother found a letter that he had written some months previously, when he knew he was going to die and had had one of those almost 'out of the body' experiences. She was not meant to find the letter until after his death. Part of it was as follows:

> When I was told, I had no sense of shock or fear. I do not remember a time when I was afraid of death, that is apart from being afraid of the trauma which goes with that transition. Nor had I any regrets for the things I was leaving. The things of the world faded into insignificance then, if I thought of them at all. As I lay there, I felt I was moving into something infinitely great and all-embracing. It was as if I was entering a new existence that was so great and wonderful that it could not be held in the old. The

things I believed, the doctrines of the faith, my understanding of God's way for me, and His world, were far too small and narrow to hold what lay before me, or what I was realising even then. It was not that these things were not true, but they were tiny vessels that could not now hold what I was being given to know. It was as if I was on the threshold of the great 'knowing'.

It seems to me that, in some sense, heaven is very near, and that when we reach that destination, all the things that have been pure and lovely and good, sheer gift in this life, especially maybe relationships (those that have meant the most) will be recognisable, but with infinitely more beauty. So, for those whom we have loved – and some would say 'loved and lost' – not so. They have not gone far away. They have gone to God, and God is very near.

For ourselves, whatever stage of the journey we are at, the important thing is really to live right now, to savour the journey with all of our heart, soul, mind and strength, to look forward to what is up ahead with a song on our lips and a prayer in our hearts, and to trust that before we even realise we're there, a pair of arms will go around us, someone will kiss us on the cheek, and the 'Leader' along with the now visible crowd of witnesses will say 'Welcome home!'

Until that time comes, my prayer is to travel well, to believe that the farther shore is reachable from here, and always to have the courage and the openness to cross the range to see.

PART TWO

GOD SPEAKS ON THE WAY

INTRODUCTION

As I have journeyed over the last years, there have been particular points at which I have felt clearly that God has spoken. When I sought to put on paper what I believed I was hearing, what appeared was in the form of reflective poetry. I have a strong sense that these reflections have been 'given' because I was never able to write them to order. At certain times they just seemed to be there. I believe they were God-given. As printed here, they are in no particular order, with the exception of the epilogue. They emerged largely out of my own life experience of being part of Northern Ireland during the last thirty-one years, and out of my spiritual journey, which is inextricably linked with that experience.

They also spring from an unshakeable belief that Ireland has a destiny under God that has yet to be fulfilled. That destiny centres around the call to reconciliation. In fact, I believe that that call to the ministry of reconciliation, to be peacemakers, is the chief call of God to those of every tradition in Ireland who profess to be Christian. Because of what has been happening here, not only over the last thirty-one years, but sporadically throughout the centuries, and because, simplistically, other parts of the world have seen the 'Troubles' as a religious war, we have caused the name Christian to be an object of scorn and division.

We still have time, although it is running out, to turn that lie on its head and to beam another message around the world; one of acceptance, of mutual hospitality, of forgiveness, of peace with justice, of a love that creates room enough for all. The road to such a goal is a hard one, a costly one, often an unpopular one. But it is possible, and each person has within them (could it but be released)

what it takes to travel that road. The reflections in this book deal
with such a call, such a challenge, with the joy and the pain, and with
the deep conviction that 'one small flame is all it takes to let the
darkness know it cannot win'.

I LIGHT A CANDLE

Every day in Restoration House at noon, we stop whatever we are doing, and gather around the kitchen table. We light a candle and we pray:

> for peace in the world,
> for peace in Ireland,
> for all those who contact us asking us for prayer.

It's such a little, little thing to do, but in some sense it is the heartbeat of our life and ministry, and links us with many beloved sisters and brothers around the world, makers of peace, friends of God.

Very often throughout the last years people have said of the conflict in Ireland, 'It's too big. There is nothing I can do that will make any difference.' That statement anaesthetises any further action. It clouds our vision and reduces us to a state of self-justifiable apathy. I believe that the day of big demonstrations is behind us, and that we are in the day of small things. One little act, anointed by the Spirit, could turn this island, this world, upside-down. It has already done so in the coming of 'little' Jesus.

One day, back in 1955, a little black woman got onto a bus in Montgomery, Alabama. She was tired, not only from her current work, but tired of the oppression and segregation of many long years. So she sat down at the front of the bus, the area reserved for white people. Her action eventually caused the United States Supreme Court to rule on the unconstitutionality of bus segregation, and was the inspiration for Martin Luther King Junior to take his campaign for civil rights onto a very public stage. The woman's name was Rosa Parks. Some time later, when she was involved in the civil rights marches, someone asked her if she wasn't tired. She replied, 'Ma feet is tired, but ma soul is marchin'!'

Such a little, little thing – to sit down in a bus, to say a prayer, to stretch out a hand of friendship. Or is it?

In Ireland, as in many other parts of the world, the feet of the peacemakers are tired, but thank God many souls are still marchin'. They believe that one small flame is all it takes to let the darkness know it cannot win.

I LIGHT A CANDLE

I light a candle
and suddenly
the world about me
changes.
I am reminded
yet again
that one small flame

is all it takes
to let the darkness know
it cannot win.
I light a candle
and I see
the shadows of the centuries
flee;
the fear, suspicion
and mistrust,
the lack of love,
the hatred
and the holding on
to hurts
that multiply themselves
into darkness
so terrible and deep
it seems as if
no ray of hope
can penetrate.

I light a candle
and instantly
it becomes
a living thing
that in the stillness
speaks of welcome
and acceptance
and hospitality
and room enough
for all.

I light a candle
and I know
that fighting
against the dark
is not the answer,
but rather
to lay down
all the efforts
to hold it back,
to choose to enter
the heart of it
and surrender
to the Light
of one small flame.

For unto us
a Child is born,
God's candle
in the dark;
and suddenly,
quietly
and everlastingly
the world is
changed.

Lord, help me
to be
a candle
in the dark,
a tiny flame
that draws

its life
from You,
and bravely
burns,
knowing that
however dark
it seems
the light still shines,
and no darkness
will ever
put it out.

And so —
I light a candle,
and I know
that Jesus Christ,
Light of the World,
is present with me
NOW.

DEORA DÉ *(TEARS OF GOD)*

One of the most distinguishing and beautiful marks of the Irish countryside, especially towards the West, are the fuchsia hedges. Even for the most casual observer, they catch the eye again and again, a combination of bright red and purple against a backdrop of deep green. They are everywhere, along country roads, separating fields, nestling around farmhouses and cottages. Each little flower is perfectly made, beautifully crafted. Each one looks as if, at any moment, it will drop from its branch to the waiting earth below. And as summer gives way to autumn, so it happens, carpeting the ground with startling colour. The Irish language gives these flowers (as it gives so many other things) a beautiful name. It calls them *Deora Dé* – the tears of God.

In the summer of 1995 and in the years since then, I have been struck by the profusion of bloom on the fuchsia hedges, and by the brightness of their colour. It is as if they are trying to speak, to convey a message. The words of St Paul in Romans Chapter 8:21-22 come instantly to mind: 'All creation anticipates the day when it will join God's children in glorious freedom from death and decay. For we know that all of creation has been groaning as in the pains of childbirth right up to the present time.' And it seems to me that just as long ago Jesus wept over the Holy City, so today he weeps over Ireland – so divided; over His world – so broken; over His Church – so often ineffective. In the absence of any prophetic voice, the *Deora Dé* speak for those with eyes to see and ears to hear.

DEORA DÉ (TEARS OF GOD)

Beautiful profusion,
silently blooming,
falling, falling
endlessly
from green hedge
to waiting earth,
this thirsty earth,
this Ireland,
that soaks up
the tears of God,
and asks
for more
and more.

And so the flowers
bloom and fall,
part of all creation
groaning,
eagerly longing
that we might awaken
to a new freedom;

a freedom
that has nothing
to do
with violence
or scoring points;
with politics
or measured words,
but a freedom
that comes
from hearts and minds
transformed,
open to each other,
learning to love,
willing to risk,
embracing vulnerability,
welcoming difference,
part of the journey
to deeper unity
and celebration.

And still the flowers
bloom and fall,
silently waiting
for a voice to cry
'Enough! Enough!
It is enough!'
Too many tears,
too much blood shed
not once on Calvary
but ever and again
as the Heart of God
aches and breaks

over His world,
over Ireland,
over His Church;
and we,
unseeing
and unheeding,
we, His body,
limp along
cautiously
leading from behind,
so far behind,
imprisoned
by the fears
of years,
by ignorance
and arrogance,
by lack of faith,
by vision marred
that does not see
the flowers bloom
and fall,
that cannot hear
the tears of God,
or sense
the unquenchable
and burning
thirst
of a land
so wounded
and so divided
that only the brokenness

of a God
who weeps
and breaks
and dies
and rises
can mend
and heal;
and so the flowers
bloom and fall.

How long, O Lord,
how long
until we see
and stoop to gather up
these precious
falling blooms,
and having drunk
ourselves
have life
to offer
that will slake
the thirst,
and cause
a people
to rise up
in joy
and gratitude,
owning the God,
who for love
of them
has let the flowers
bloom and fall?

THAT THEY MAY BE ONE

How much we in the body of Christ need each other! How much we have to give and to receive from each other! How little we recognise that! How defensively we cling to our particular beliefs, guarding our patch against all comers! How afraid we are of acknowledging that no one denomination is sole possessor of the truth! And how often we use the Week of Prayer for Christian Unity as our annual conscience salver.

Increasingly, I have a deep sense of awe as I read and reflect on the Gospel of John, Chapter 17, where we are given the enormous privilege of listening in to one of the very last prayers Jesus prayed before He died. It was the most central, the most important cry of His heart. And He prayed it, not only for the disciples, His friends who were with Him, but also for all those who would believe in Him because of their testimony. And that means (unrestricted now by time and space) that Jesus, Son of God, was and is praying for us. And what is still, therefore, the cry of His Heart? It is very simply that we might be one. Not so that we could have a cosy, holy huddle together, but that we might be one so that the world would believe.

Isn't it rather strange that the Church has ignored that prayer for so long? We tend to be very selective about what we give allegiance to in terms of our faith. We readily agree to those things that we can carry out within the confines of our own traditions, our concept of what it's all about. But at the core of the Christian faith is a 'yes', not to doctrine, dogma, or tradition, but to Person, the Person of Jesus Himself. And a 'yes' to Him means an engagement of our whole beings, our whole selves. That 'yes' will lead us on many journeys, some of which may run directly counter to our cherished notions of things. It's not that He's asking us to become all the same. That would be very boring. But He is asking us to be united in purpose, in witness, in love; to be that prophetic voice that will cause weary hearts to beat again with expectancy, and drooping heads to rise again in hope, and tired feet to stride out again on the journey of faith.

Right now it's time to risk. And if courage fails, if we wonder what effect one little action on our part would have, if we feel like running again to the womb of how things have always been, let's pick up John 17 and keep it by us. Let's draw strength and determination from the One who – so soon to be isolated, betrayed, rejected, killed, in order that we might be reconciled to God and to each other – prayed that earnest prayer as one of His last pleas to the Father, and is still praying that for us. Wouldn't it be so good to be part of the answer, rather than part of the question?

Sometimes we are given the great gift of meeting someone from a different tradition, another culture, with whom we sense immediate harmony. As we risk and grow in relationship, it is as if we have always known each other and there flows the sense of each being deeply a part of the one worldwide family of God. The friendship, held in the heart of Jesus, becomes like a little icon of what God desires for His Church – a unity in diversity, an acceptance of difference, a mutual hospitality, a willingness to be open and vulnerable, a generosity of spirit, a love that has nothing to do with defensiveness or possessiveness, but that is liberating and encouraging. And, although times of meeting may be few, when they do happen they are eternity moments, during which we are given food for the journey and wine for rejoicing.

THAT THEY MAY BE ONE

And it must always be so,
this joy and this pain,
this balm and this ache,
this ecstasy and this agony,
this hello and this goodbye,
this holding and this letting go,
this coming home and this setting out;
not knowing where we're going, and yet
knowing that we go with God,
and that the same God travels
with you and with me,
and the journey is the same,
though we embrace, and you go one way
and I the other,
yet not divided,
only deeper communion
beyond the sadness.
The paradox of missing you
because you are not here,
and yet not missing you
because you are ever present;

this vulnerability gladly welcomed
because it welcomes you;
this knowledge that both are held
in the heart of Jesus;
this sense of wonder at His love
who could, unasked,
pour out such gift;
who lets us see His heart,
a heart that aches and yearns
for unity
and then invites us in
and lets us rest together
in communion,
giving strength
that we might again
pick up the mantle
of 'pilgrim'
in this love
held in His love;
love that gives
food for the journey
and wine for rejoicing.
And when the road is hard,
the night is long;
when all seems weariness,
brokenness,
anguish;
when the violence of what
people do to each other
and to themselves
assumes the proportion

of a monster;
when sometimes the spectres
of horror
become reality,
and the tears of God
fall heavily
unseen by many;
when our own brokenness
and littleness
take control,
anaesthetise,
immobilise;
when 'self' usurps the throne
and issues the decrees
'You can't',
'It is impossible',
and asks the mocking question
'Who are you?'
When all seems dark
and no light shines;
when even the dearest
human communion
seems mirage,
and the silent scream
'Where are you?'
fills the universe;
when trust is shattered
in a thousand pieces,
and the octopus of fear
coils its tentacles
around the gut of being;

when that 'Body of Christ',
that instrument of God,
that Beauty and that Beast
imposes more
numerous
and self-inflicted wounds,
increasing blindness,
deafness,
paralysis;
so that this broken Body,
becoming so disfigured,
is scarcely recognisable;
when wounds are
not exposed
and treated;
when there is
no cleansing
through repentance
and forgiveness,
no pouring in
of oil of compassion;
when the superficial dressing
of 'all is well',
of 'let's pray together
once, or maybe several times
a year'
conceals temporarily
the deep infection;
and when, stress increasing
reveals the open
oozing sores

of disunity
and self-righteousness
and hardness of heart;
when all seems
impassable gulf,
and there are no bridges;
when the only prayer,
all doctrine
and dogma
and theology
disappearing,
is 'O God!
O God...!'
Then somewhere
in that abyss of nothingness
a bridge appears,
strange engineering,
extravagant shape,
straining and stretching
across that gulf
of disunity,
while below
the demons
of division
swirl and scream
across;
a cross.
Is not the cross a bridge?
And once again
we are back
to the beginning

where we started
in the heart of Jesus,
knowing that the
unity
for which His heart yearns,
for which His body
was strained and stretched
across the gulf,
is already won,
is here,
is ours
to claim;
and the claiming
is for us to be
little pilgrims of unity;
to allow ourselves
to be strained and stretched
across the gulf
of broken relationships;
offering our own
brokenness
to Him
that in Him
we too (we two)
may be a bridge,
across which
others may meet
and greet
and know themselves
one
and 'at home'
together in Him.

A HAND OF FRIENDSHIP

Ireland is plagued with anniversaries commemorating 'old, unhappy, far off things, and battles long ago'.[1] The stories and the memories passed down to us lose nothing in the telling. If not addressed, their drumbeat in our communal ancestral gut grows ever stronger. They are for us precious treasure, often becoming the impetus for further negative action in the present. And so history repeats itself, with each scenario adding fuel to the seemingly inextinguishable flame of division and sectarianism.

In 1998 we were commemorating yet another anniversary, that of the 1798 Rebellion of the United Irishmen. Up until that time Presbyterians and Catholics in Ireland had much in common, having the same Penal Laws enacted against them. There are many historical accounts of their support for one another. Rather than celebrate a rebellion, we in Restoration Ministries decided to do something positive, namely to encourage the two traditions to rediscover a friendship that had existed in times of adversity.

---

1. William Wordsworth, 'The Solitary Reaper', in *Selected Poems* (London: Penguin, 1996), p. 169.

The idea was very little, with no hidden agenda, and totally apolitical. We encouraged an individual or a family from one tradition to invite an individual or a family from the other tradition into their home for a cup of coffee or a simple meal. This stemmed from the basic belief that there is something intimate and relationship-building in breaking bread together. Ireland will be changed not so much by political agreements, important as they are, but by the forming of relationships upon which change of attitude depends.

We called our project A Hand of Friendship. While the focus in the anniversary year was on Presbyterians and Catholics, we were hopeful that the idea would spread to all traditions.

So small a thing to ask — and yet so big: 'Give me your hand.'

A HAND OF FRIENDSHIP

If your heart is for peace,
And my heart is for peace,
Give me your hand.

Give me your hand,
so small a thing to ask,
and yet — so big.

If I let my hand
touch
       grasp
              clasp

your hand,
then somehow

I have crossed
the Rubicon;
I cannot be the same.
I cannot be the same
if, in the clasping
of your hand,
I dare to raise
my head
and look into your eyes,
and see a mirror image
of myself,
frightened of trusting,
fearful of the unknown,
scared to admit
your humanity,
to be open and vulnerable,
lest I am invaded,
taken over,
lest all 'they'
have told me
over centuries
proves to be
true
about you.

Give me your hand.
O give me your hand
before the moment passes,
before the darkness overtakes,
and I discover
when it is too late,

that you were my sister,
you were my brother,
that together
we were being called
towards a future
bright with hope
and promise,
by the God
whose hand
forever reaches out
to you and me
in friendship,
and because of whom
we can never be the same.

And so,
may the peace of Christ
be with you,
and may He ever flow
between us
as I
give you
my hand.

THE WELCOME

During Advent 1995, I visited Trosly, a little village north-east of Paris, for the first time. It was here, thirty years previously, that Jean Vanier invited two men, Raphael and Philippe, from a long-term mental institution to come and live in community with him. From these small beginnings has grown a worldwide movement which we know as L'Arche, meaning the ark, the place of safety. The ethos of L'Arche is that it is the people with learning disabilities, the poor and the little who are special, who are the beloved. They also are God's gift to us, in that they reveal to us the truth about ourselves, namely that we are all poor and little and broken, but that we too are beloved.

In the initial hours of that first visit, I remember I felt very isolated. My knowledge of French was minimal. I didn't know anyone, and my whole desire was to turn around and go home. In that frame of mind, I went to the chapel where, every evening, communities from the different foyers gather for Mass. I sat down on my own. After a little while the door opened and a man entered. Out of all the places he could have gone, he came and sat by me. He didn't say anything. He just took my hand and kissed me on the

cheek. All through the liturgy he held my hand and kissed me. I felt
so welcomed. His name was Bernard. He happens to have Down's
Syndrome. He has become someone who is very dear to my heart.
He epitomises for me that hospitality that is at the core of the
Gospel. This hospitality so needs to be restored in the Body of
Christ, in order that a broken, weary, warring, hopeless world may
be encouraged, may believe that it, too, is loved and accepted, and
may come home to God.

THE WELCOME (*FOR BERNARD*)

You had not encountered me before,
you could not speak,
you did not know my name
and yet, you welcomed me.

You had no words,
you could not 'write it down',
you could not 'think it out',
and yet, you welcomed me.

And, sitting down, you took my hand,
you lifted up your face to kiss my cheek
and waited for the answer.
And so, you welcomed me.

Strange weapons these
to break down all defences,
disarming me, before I knew.
That's how you welcomed me.

Caution would tell me
'Let the head control'.
But I have learned a wisdom
in the way you welcomed me.

Your heart could see
the handicap in me,
and, reaching out, embrace it
in the way you welcomed me.

And, in that risk of faith
in reaching out to me,
you made me feel at home,
as in trust you welcomed me.

Brokenness, littleness, communion,
all were there,
because you gave yourself
to welcome me.

Your heart reached out to me
and wonder grew,
as you called forth from me
a wordless welcome too.

Our lives are drowned in many words
that don't seem real.
But, in your self I heard the Word
that welcomed me.

MAGNIFICAT

Throughout the ages there have been many different expectations about God breaking into His world afresh, and doing mighty things. This is especially so at key points in history, as, for example, at the turn of a century or the passing from one millennium to another. But how do we expect God to come? How do we imagine He will act?

Mary has so much to show us about the nature of God's coming. The soul who magnifies the Lord is there for God to work through. This is always the point where God breaks into the experience of people. Out of humble adoration and a listening heart, their 'yes' emerges, as Mary's did. Hers was a yes that was to change the history of humanity; a yes through which the lives of countless millions were to be redeemed. That yes opened the door for the light that no darkness can master to shine in our world. It was a yes that has caused all generations to call her blessed, and yet caused sorrow like a sharp sword to pierce her own heart.

Many outside the Catholic and Orthodox traditions have missed much in their over-reaction to what they believe to be wrong doctrine. Mary is the wonderful proof in herself that God's way of coming is not dependent upon the great of this world. Rather, He delights to act through the unknown and the humble. Worldly estimation and values count for little in His scheme of things. Mary highlights for us the truth that 'God deliberately chose men and women that the culture overlooks and exploits and abuses, chose those "nobodies" to expose the hollow pretensions of the "somebodies" '.[1]

I sense that in the hearts of many people today, there is a deep and hidden longing for such awareness, in a world where power reigns supreme, and the poor are trampled into the dust. Yet, how slow we still are to look for the coming God among the displaced, the little, the vulnerable, the poor of the earth.

It is here, among the least of these, that, if we seek, we will find a new 'yes' emerging. That yes is heard through communities of compassion and forgiveness, through prophetic voices, through lights shining in dark places, through many little signs of hope and love. Here, God is breaking through – right now.

MAGNIFICAT

I am Mary –
young, so young;
child of peasant stock;
native of unknown Nazareth;
descendant of Abraham;
member of a race
subjected over the long years
to hardship, oppression, war, exile, poverty;

---

1. Eugene H. Peterson, '1 Corinthians 1:27-28', *The Message* (Colorado Springs: Navapress, 1994), p. 403.

one of those who prays continually
with her people
'Lord, how long?'
and who hopes, with them,
for the coming
of God's Messiah.
The years grind on,
and sorrow through the centuries
like a sharp sword
has pierced our nation's heart.

I am Mary –
bethrothed to Joseph,
good man and faithful;
my life laid out for me
like that of any other woman of Nazareth
until the messenger comes;
and though in turmoil,
though full of apprehension,
fears and misgivings,
though I do not understand,
I choose to trust the One
who sends the message,
and to receive into my being
the life
that will bring light
to all the world.
My soul magnifies the Lord,
and my spirit rejoices
in God, my saviour.
And yet, I know

that sorrow,
like a sharp sword,
will pierce my heart.

I am Mary –
the faces of those years
pass before me now;
the heavenly visage of Gabriel,
the joyful incredulity of Elizabeth,
the wisdom and caring of Joseph,
the tired harassment and concern
of the innkeeper,
the wonder and adoration
of the shepherds,
the humility of the great
in the expression of the kings,
the impassioned cruelty
of Herod's soldiers,
the foreign features of Egypt,
the extreme old age and worship
of Simeon and Anna;
and, above all and through it all,
the face of the Child.
I live again
the emotions of those years;
the expectation, the awe,
the happiness,
the pain and fear,
the homelessness,
the flight and exile,
the earthly hiddenness of His coming,

and the heavenly declaration of joy.
And already this heart
knows a piercing,
as though with a sharp sword,
of sorrow and rejoicing.

I am Mary —
I remember the blessed
silent years of Nazareth;
the guiding and the growing,
the work and the play;
the never-to-be-forgotten
Passover in Jerusalem,
and then,
central to all motherhood
since time began,
the letting go;
realisation that this Child,
as all,
is gift for just a little while,
not possession.

The letting go
to the way prepared
before all ages,
the way that leads
to where I stand
before this cross,
and hear His words,
for me, for me.
All other words,

for all other people,
for time and for eternity,
but these words – for me:

'Woman, behold your Son,
Son behold your mother.'

Sorrow
like a sharp sword,
has pierced my heart.
And yet
in the midst of darkness
I hear the consummation cry
'It is finished'.
So that, even now
my soul magnifies the Lord
and my spirit rejoices
in God, my saviour.

I am Mary –
blessed among many;
celebrating resurrection victory;
and once again,
as I did so long ago,
but now at Pentecost,
receiving into my life
His life,
so that,
together with countless others
throughout the ages,
we might bear His life
to the world.

THE HARD CHOICE

Life is filled with choices. Every day we make hundreds of them, but they become so familiar that we are really not aware that that is what we are doing. Every choice excludes others naturally, and each one has its own consequences. The freedom to choose is the biggest gift God gave us when He made us. Perhaps the most crucial choices are in our reactions to events and to people. Many don't even recognise that they are presented with choices here. They simply react out of their current or ancestral gut feeling. But for those who have been awakened to the reality of Jesus in their lives, this freedom to choose how we react is an awesome responsibility.

Lent means different things to different people, but maybe beyond everything else, as we seek to be with and to follow Jesus, it is the season of hard choices. It's the time when we prepare ourselves for costly service, service that will lead us along the Jerusalem road. Whoever we are, it's the hard choices that shape our lives, and not only ours, but also the lives of those around us and further afield, even the lives of generations yet unborn. There is no escaping the agony of hard choosing, as we sense Jesus calling us to go deeper, to travel further with Him. We've seen the vision, we've glimpsed the goal, we've heard the call. But the way in part leads through alien territory. No easy journey this, rather a road of danger, of misunderstanding, a road along which lurk the powers of darkness seeking to scatter, destroy and rob those who travel it. There comes the point in every life of faith where, seeing the reality, we have to make up our minds, to set our faces – and go.

This is true for Christians everywhere, but especially, I believe, for us in Ireland in these days. We are in a special time of opportunity that will not last forever, and the eyes of the world are upon us to see how we are living it. What image of Christianity, of Jesus, is being beamed around the world from Ireland today? Is it the same as that of the thirty years of the Troubles, or is something different happening? If we have anything at all to offer out of the nightmare of the past, if we have anything of hope to give, it is in the ministry of reconciliation. That is what will make others sit up and take notice – when they see Christian people who have been at loggerheads with each other for so long now standing together, restoring the waste places created by bigotry, mistrust, fear and unforgiveness, being united in witness, in purpose, in love. That also is what would delight the heart of God, and cause Him to open the windows of heaven and pour down blessings upon this fragile, rebellious, wounded land. The call to the ministry of reconciliation is top of Jesus' agenda for the Churches in Ireland. Sadly, it is not yet top of theirs. There have been messengers, not enough, but some sent ahead to prepare the way. In many instances they have not been accepted or heard. But now is the crucial time for us to respond to this call, to choose to go this way, before it is too late.

THE HARD CHOICE

Jesus set his face.
What does it mean for me
to set my face,
to make the hard choice,
to take the road less travelled?
I try to work it out,
to see the end from the beginning,
to calculate the risks involved,
to manage ways of self-protection
just in case they're needed,
to tread warily among the time-bombs
of prejudice and hatred,
of rejection and bitterness,
of self-righteousness and anger,
of fear fired by half-truth
and unexploded myths.

I take such tiny steps,
like some reluctant pilgrim,
my face not set,
but ever looking right and left
and backwards,
deliberating if another little step
is possible,
weighing up the pros and cons,
desperately seeking affirmation
and companionship
along the way.

Jesus set His face.
He calls for us
to come with Him,
the way for us made possible
because He walked it first,
because at journey's end for Him
were arms outstretched
in isolating welcome
of wood and nails;
because to such embrace
He yielded
in obedience and in love,
so that we may travel bravely
in similar obedience
and all-embracing love
among the time-bombs of our fears,
and know the victory
along the way;
and at the end
find – not a cross –
but Jesus' arms
outstretched
to welcome us.

THIS TIME

God's people are always people of destiny, of purpose. Most of the time we don't recognise that fact, and therefore don't seek to fulfil it. Part of the difficulty is that we gather to ourselves so much baggage that seems to us impossible to shift. So we settle down in the middle of it all, and any thoughts of anything different, any vision for journeying, any sense of risk or adventure leave us.

There is a story told of Columba, that on one occasion a traveller was visiting the saint in his cell on Iona. The traveller looked around at the bare little place, at its spartan conditions, and said to Columba:

'Where is your furniture?'
'Where's yours?' replied Columba.
'Mine?' said the traveller. 'But I'm just passing through.'
'So am I,' said Columba.

The furniture or baggage can be so many things. Along with the normal things we gather to ourselves during a lifetime, in Ireland we are also cluttered and weighed down by attitudes passed down through the generations, hooking us into denominational, sectarian or political imprisonment or idolatries of various sorts. Within each of us there are deep and frightening things that trap us and render us seemingly powerless to move forward. We make sorties out, but again and again are pulled back to the same place.

Yet, there is a time for every purpose under heaven. From somewhere in these days there is coming the gentle but authoritative challenge: 'Now is the time for the real work of reconciliation to begin.' Now, when the killing, the destruction, the maiming has stopped, all the hurt of the years, the questioning as to the point of it all, is coming to the surface. There are so many silent screams needing to be given voice, so many stories to be heard, so much pain to be felt before it can be laid down, so much recognition that repentance and forgiveness are themselves a journey that will take a long time, an ongoing process of going deeper and deeper.

It is so important that we don't remain tied to the moorings of yesterday, but that we risk launching out. This is not to dismiss everything in our lives that has gone before, that has shaped and moulded and stretched us, that has made us into the people we are today. But it is about recognising God's moment. It is about responding in obedience and trust. And it's going to mean leaving so much that is familiar behind. It's going to mean responding to the call to love with all the passion and the folly of Jesus, being icons of hope in a world nearly drowning in despair. It's going to mean becoming makers, rather than lovers of peace, which will often push us to the margins into the surprising company of those friends of God who, in the upside-down nature of His Kingdom, are called blessed when they are persecuted for righteousness' sake. And we are called to travel this way with joy.

Into our lives, at some point, comes this request or command of Jesus. We cannot ask others to do it if we are not prepared to go that way ourselves, to put our lives where our words have been. And the outer reflects the inner. The biggest reconciliation journey I have to travel is within myself, where there are still so many fears and doubts and prejudices, and lack of love. It's the one that demands the most. If I have braved that sea, I can brave any other storm.

The Irish conflict is among the oldest in the world. Somehow under God we need to assume the responsibility of advancing years, to do something and be something that will cause others with younger conflicts to stop, to look, to listen, to ask questions – and be given hope. As we have caused the name of Christian to be an object of scorn and derision over the years, so through the grace and mercy of God, and through the faithfulness of many hidden people, that could yet be turned upside-down. People could once again say: 'See how these Christians love one another!' Time is running out, but Ireland still has that chance. Could it be that this is our time?

THIS TIME

To everything a season,
a time for every purpose under heaven,
and yet this time
out of all other times
is special.
A moment of grace,
a Kairos time,
a time of urgency
when there is no time;
a window opened on eternity
where all is possible
for those with eyes to see
and ears to hear

and hearts to understand.
A time to risk
all that has not been risked
before
so that we might flow
with all that God intends.
A time to seize
because it will not come
again.
A time to place
our lives
where words have been.
A time for bridges
to be built
and others crossed,
and others burned,
because there is
no going back.
A time to leave
the past behind
because the present,
this precious 'now',
is Holy Ground
and from it
the future beckons.
To leave the past,
but not to do so
lightly.
To take it out
and dare to look
and name

what has been done
and cannot be undone.

To allow the pain
to surface.
To give voice
to silent wounding,
that, hearing,
and being heard,
we might
with due and holy reverence
allow the dying
to take place,
and, picking up
the pieces that give life,
to travel on;
our burden now
a cleansed
and sanctified inheritance;
one that puts into our step
a spring
and into our hearts
a flame of hope
that cannot be extinguished.

This time
so fragile
and so priceless,
gift of God
to you and me
to grasp

and to embrace,
to give it
all we've got;
and, in the giving
and receiving,
to learn to celebrate
the Presence
of the One
who in His mercy
and His grace
has given
one more time.

SONG WITHOUT WORDS

'If these Christians want me to believe in their god, they'll have to sing me better songs, they'll have to look more like people who have been saved; they'll have to wear on their countenance the joy of the beatitudes. I could only believe in a god who dances.' So wrote Nietzsche, the philosopher who said that God is dead. Songs worth singing, people rescued and journeying towards home, radiation of joy, a dancing God. Is that what others catch when they encounter us? Sometimes there are no songs at all, only a funeral dirge as we inwardly mourn for those parts of our beings that are dead or in exile. Each of us has a shadow side and a light side. Each of us, for various reasons, but usually in order, so we think, to survive and cope, has to a greater or lesser degree repressed much of the shadow. Sometimes when we allow some of these things to surface to consciousness, they can threaten to take us over, so much so that our whole being seems to be in exile. We echo the cry of the psalmist: 'Here in exile my heart is breaking.' And I suppose it's true that a bit of our heart is always breaking, because we are never fully 'at home' within ourselves this side of death. The part of us that is in control, the 'adult' part, taunts us in the way the Israelites were taunted by their Babylonian captors long ago: 'Sing us one of the songs of Zion.' And from the shadows, the exiled part, the wounded child cries out: 'How can we sing the Lord's song in a foreign land?' Yet, all the time our God is waiting. He has a better song, a new song for us to sing, a song that will attract others, but in our exiled state we can't hear it, or catch the tune, or pick up the beat.

We say of ourselves and of others: 'This is all there is. This is me. That is her or him.' Yet every human being is a mystery. I can never say I know another person fully, because that would be to write them off, to relegate them to something less than human, to box or label them, to place restrictions on their ability to grow, to change, to become. There is always more to us than our normal experience of ourselves. Each one of us is a complex, many-levelled reality.

Did you ever think that every sense of something more, every stretch of thought, every flash of inspiration, every thought of greater good is as much a part of you as the genetic base from which you came? That just as you remember some of those forces in your early life that have shaped you and made you, so this something more that causes within you an aching and yearning is, in a sense, the homesickness of a heart that is remembering from where it came and to where it is going?

When we feel these things, somewhere we are remembering, we are hearing more clearly, a note that is finer, purer than the ancient drumbeat of our divided history, stirring us at a level that is deeper even than our ancestral gut. It has its origin in where we came from, from the Heart of God, from a place beyond memory, and it calls us forward to risk travelling to that place from whence we came, to travel home. But we must do it together.

We shall not cease from exploration
And the end of all our exploring
Will be to arrive where we started
And know the place for the first time. [1]

Somewhere within each of us we may have had a flash or a glimpse of something we would love to do as part of God's peace process for Ireland or for the world. In that split second, it has seemed gloriously possible and vaguely familiar. And then, out of our own brokenness and woundedness that listens so readily to the negative, to the voices that say 'you can't', we bury it again. Yet, for one instant, the depths of our being were touched by the snatch of a tune, by a refrain that was old but ever new.

Is the call to dare to believe that there is more than we can see? Is it to risk hearing something different than what has been fed to us, what we've taken on board over the years, and then to go for it?

There is a song – to hear and to sing. Maybe as yet we haven't heard it very clearly. But it's there – and it's a song from home – from the Heart of God.

SONG WITHOUT WORDS

Play it again.
O play it again.
There is something there
that I remember,
a fleeting melody,
a snatch of tune,

1. T. S. Eliot, 'Little Gidding', *Four Quartets* (London: Faber & Faber Ltd, 1959), p. 48.

an old refrain,
that calls forth
from the depths of me
a chord so moving,
so clothed in beauty,
so much in harmony,
something without words
that is eternal,
remembered
from another time,
another place,
and yet recognised
as being
part of me
and part of you;
yet, paradoxically,
beyond the two;
a song that comes
from the heart
of One
whose life
sings life
and love
and peace
for all the world,
and you and me;
a song that
gives us
to each other
that we might
sing this song
for all the world.
O play it again!

A SECOND DEATH

Most of us in our lives will go through, at least once, a time of great pain, or loneliness, or betrayal or anguish. In such a time of darkness, the first security to be shattered and the last one to be rebuilt afterwards is trust. Of its very nature, trust is fragile. In such a time, there is often an endless, aching need for reassurance, acceptance, a need to be cherished for who one is. These can become insatiable hungers in the dark night that is all-embracing. The battered and buffeted pilgrim, seeking to stand or to travel through such a time of desolation, experiences not death itself, but what seems like a dying process. In some small sense she is suffering a silent, screaming agony, a 'garden' anguish, while others seem to sleep. The cry of the heart is for God to take this 'thing' away. But, instead, the darkness increases, the enemy creeps in closer and, often under the guise of love, betrays. The pilgrim is bound and powerless, burdened down, unjustly accused. The night is lonely, the road too long. Weariness threatens to overcome her. The cry of dereliction rises to her lips. And yet, somewhere deep within, there is a seed waiting to become, waiting to be nourished once again by the warm sun of love. It is a seed that, through all the bitter snows that have heaped themselves layer upon layer upon it, still says 'yes' to life, to growth, to becoming all that God intends.

If we have ever been on such a pilgrimage, we will know what a precious gift it has been to have with us those who have assured us that we're going to make it, those who have lifted the burden when it has been too heavy and carried it awhile, those who have stood and prayed, those who have dared to look and smile in the dark night. Through such sharing, through some strange yet intimate grace, we recognise that we, too, are numbered among the ranks of Good Friday people. We are encouraged to make the choice to go on and on until it is finished – and only just begun.

It is equally important for others to be there in love as we emerge. They can be image-bearers of Jesus for us, if they recognise that what they touch in us is holy ground, made such through suffering. We are vulnerable and fragile. If the clouds gather and the winds of adversity blow too quickly, if what is offered is withdrawn too soon, there can be a second death.

What a challenge and a call to the Body of Christ – to grow in sensitivity and compassion, as we, in our own fragility, seek to be present with and for others whose hearts have been wounded, and whose trust has been shattered.

And when we can bring our brokenness together, even for an instant, Jesus is surely present.

A Second Death

You came in love,
and with warm gentleness
and words of healing balm
you soothed this wounded heart;
and in the midst of shattered trust,
you planted deep within
a seed I never thought to know again;
and, risking plant and nurturing,
I dared to let the roots go down
deep into the soil of love;
and slowly, oh so slowly,
there appeared a tiny shoot
that grew and grew,
until one day
a bud appeared
that symbolised new trust and hope;
a daring to believe
that here in this poor soul
was something worthy of such love.
And the little bud,
so timidly yet bravely,
risked and straightened
and greeted the new day,
and opened up
a petal here, a petal there,
and the warm sun of love
created confidence
that all was well.
But then, one day a cloud appeared

and blotted out the warmth
and caused chill winds to blow
and harsh rain to fall,
that bruised and shook the tender plant
and broke the petals off,
and caused the bud to close up,
oh, so tightly,
all remaining bloom,
and bend its head
and vainly try
to disappear once more
into the dark earth from whence it came,
never again to flower.
But there was no going back;
only a dying
out in the open
for all to see.

HERALD OF THE DAWN

Very early one morning, in the month of November, I was sitting reflecting, praying, preparing myself for the day that lay waiting. Outside, the chilly pitch-blackness was rendered more menacing and sinister by the all-pervading fog. Suddenly, in the midst of the shrouded gloom and darkness, I heard a bird carolling for all it was worth. I listened in awe. And then I remembered that someone once had said: 'A bird does not sing to bring up the dawn. It sings because the dawn is coming.' After a while, the dawn broke, and I experienced a great lifting of the heart. The bird was certain that the night would soon be over and was heralding the reality of a new day.

Much of our life in the Church appears to be a waiting time. But there are different ways of waiting. We can do so passively, almost existing rather than living, or we can wait passionately, with every fibre of our being on tiptoe, expectant.

Advent is such a time. It is what I like to think of as a threshold time, a thin time where the veil between what we can see and touch and handle, and the world of mystery, of spiritual reality, is almost transparent. There is the sense of being in the company of countless others from every age who are passionately waiting for the God who comes.

But it's not only Advent. I believe that we are living in such a period at this very moment. Ireland has been a land where death has cast its shadow for far too long. It could be that way again. Continually the darkness strives to overcome the light, in individual women and men, in structures and institutions, in communities. Darkness does not give up easily. But as we wait in this threshold time, on the edge of a place we have never been before, as we stand on tiptoe, hardly daring to trust that the night is over, and lasting peace is possible, can we dare to believe that right now God is beginning again with us, offering us another chance? After so many years, can we dare to grasp that this is a fresh start, no longer with any disguise, but rather the grey cold light of a morning where, although the sun has risen, it is not yet visible behind the clouds? And, like those who have been through a long hard night where they could not sleep, it may be difficult to rise and get moving, but that is the call.

As we stand on this sort of threshold, I, for one, am somewhat overwhelmed by it, almost as if it's a bit too much. But, then, Jesus is a bit 'too much'! And maybe what this time is saying is: 'Don't close the door when it seems too much. Be open. Wait passionately in every part of your being. Sing your song, or else listen for it in the darkness. When you receive the signal, step out. As you do so, you will catch glimpses of a new day where God is.' And in the 'too muchness' of God, that is enough. It is enough to keep us going, because the unseen reality is always Emmanuel.

We are called to be heralds. If we're singing to bring up the dawn, we've missed it. But if we're singing because the dawn is coming, then let us rejoice and lift up our hearts.

HERALD OF THE DAWN

Here I am, Lord,
waiting;
waiting on the edge of the dark.
Before me
nothing
but a promise.
Behind me
the black night
of restlessness,
dereliction,
betrayal,
mourning.
How long the journey has taken
I know not.
All I know —
a pilgrim,
travel-sore and weary,
hungering and thirsting,
aching and yearning
for the dawn;
called to be herald
for other weary pilgrims;
called to be herald
of the dawn within myself;
to stake my very life
on something not yet seen,
and with reckless abandon
to open up my heart
and sing;

because – I know it's true,
because – I know it's You,
because – I know that morning comes
for those who have the courage
to wait
and hope
and
sing.

A Journey Shared

Even after nearly two thousand years of Christianity, things haven't changed all that much. Long ago the religious leaders kept questioning Jesus as to who He was. But they didn't, or couldn't, or wouldn't, recognise Him, because of closed minds and closed hearts. Jesus said to them, 'You don't believe because you are not part of my flock.' They didn't recognise His voice and follow. They thought they knew it all. And, in a sense, they did know it all. They knew their scriptures, their history, their culture and their traditions inside out, but they didn't know Jesus. This man unsettled them, spoke what to them was sacrilegious, and turned some of their cherished beliefs upside down. Their attitudes were fixed in solid religious and legalistic concrete that left no room for remembering their real calling as the pilgrim people of God. Nor did they allow any recognition of the One who called Himself the Way. They had arrived; and what they had, they held – to the bitter end. Their day would come, so they thought, but not through this blasphemer. They knew all about the Messiah, but they didn't know Him. No surrender here to the God who was reaching out to them in love.

It sounds so familiar. There's an inbuilt negativity in most of us that militates against any forward movement. God has so much more that He wants to give us, to do in us and through us, and we're never going to discover it unless we're willing to give Him a free hand. To say yes to Him at a deeper and deeper level is, in a sense, saying 'yes' to an inner peace process that will eventually powerfully affect the outer. This does not mean that life will become less, that we will lose some of our identity. Rather it means that we'll be discovering more and more who we really are. Our primary identity, that is, as daughters and sons of God, will come more clearly into focus. In recognising who we are in Him, we will become so much more deeply aware of others within the family of God, not only in Ireland, but in the rest of the British Isles and around the world. Our secondary identities, for example, our Irishness or Britishness, our Catholicism or Protestantism, our age or youth, our femaleness or maleness, our cultures – all these things we'll begin to look on as gifts to take delight in and to be shared with one another, rather than to be held on to defensively, and guarded against all comers.

There's a big world out there that we in Ireland cannot ignore any more, and many are looking at us. Much of the world's population wouldn't even have heard of this island, had it not been for the thirty years of the Troubles. Now it's universally known for its strife, and only very recently for the fragile signs of hope. We have a long way to go. But the journey is vital, and can be in itself part of the promised riches. It starts with each one of us resolving before God to go for it, in whatever way He whispers to each heart; being willing to share the parts of our journey that we feel we can share with someone else, to build each other up, to encourage each other in these precious days. When these things begin to happen, then perhaps we can be, even yet, a beacon of light and hope for other parts of the world.

A Journey Shared

These islands
set in Northern seas,
no sparkling jewels
but rather
holding deep
within their hearts
the smouldering fires
of old resentments,
of ageless hatreds
that wait eternally
to be revenged,
and claim a victory
that is bitter-sweet.

Through centuries
the fires burn;
the winds of history
fan them into flame
and then
reduce to ashes;
but still the spark remains,
ready to blaze at the first whisper
of a breath that says
'Your day has come';
and from the living embers
of yesterday,
memories old and ever new
ignite the fires
once again.

We cling to our
ancestral drumbeats
of old wounds, injustices,
betrayals
to feed our present
sense of injury;
like puppets
marching to the rhythm
of our particular drum,
unable or unwilling
to pick up
a different beat,
that calls us
not to warring marches,
but to a journey
shared,
an ancient belonging
woven intricately
through the years,
often denied,
repressed,
rejected,
but living still
for those with ears to hear.
It tells us of
a story incomplete
without each other;
a belonging older
than the heritage
we claim so proudly,
be it Celtic,

Anglo-Saxon,
Norman or Viking,
or something older still;
a belonging
that stems
from a place beyond
the memory of history;
that place
from which we came
and to which
we will return –
the Heart of God;
a God
who gives us
to each other,
and invites us
to discover
the celebration,
creativity and joy
of a journey shared,
travelling
through the years,
until the exiled
parts of us
come home
to Him.

EPILOGUE

CHRISTMAS CAME EARLY

Nothing is ever straightforward in Ireland. So often in our history we have seemed to take one step forward and two steps back, but thank God there is always something more up ahead. In the weeks leading up to Christmas 1999 so much happened in terms of the implementation of the Northern Ireland Peace Agreement, and with such a surprising degree of rapidity, that we were left awestruck, and full of gratitude. With the new Executive of the Northern Ireland Assembly in full swing, and all the various bodies operational, a surging tide of hope swept through a community that for so long had been weary and almost afraid to believe that things could be different. It is true to say that we found ourselves in a place where we had never been before, a place where it seemed that all things became possible. At the time of writing this epilogue, sadly the Executive has been suspended, there has been a return to direct rule from Westminster, and once again the fragile nature of such a peace is evident for all to see.

However, this is not a time for despair or for giving up. It is a time, as never before, for renewing hope, for being constant in prayer and for strengthening the foundations for a peaceful society in every way that we can. I am under no illusion about the difficulties ahead; there are many obstacles still to encounter, many ranges still to cross, but the belief that that farther shore is reachable from here has certainly not been diminished. In sudden flashes, in moments that are timeless, I have seen it, gift of God waiting for us, Catholic and Protestant alike, Unionist and Nationalist, male and female, old and young. But whatever happens in the coming months and years, nothing can rob us of the fact that, for us, this year, Christmas came early.

CHRISTMAS CAME EARLY

Christmas came early this year,
after seeming aeons
of waiting and watching,
of hoping and despairing,
of believing and doubting;
the God who spoke
the Word
in the beginning
and created order
out of chaos,
who spoke the Word into the darkness
of our separation
from Him
and came in Jesus,
has spoken now the Word
into our long night,
into our endless Advent
and in the midst
of seeming chaos
has created order,
has breathed His peace,
and somehow,
somewhere
along the way,
trust crept in.

Christmas came early this year;
bells ringing, hearts rejoicing;
people who before could see

only threatening shapes
looking each other in the eye
and seeing now
a human face
with a likeness
to their own;
politicians who before would have
borne the brunt
of one another's scorn
and laughter
that was demonic,
sharing jokes,
sitting around
one table,
working together
for the good of all;
governments changing
the course of history
in the twinkling of an eye,
signing away
long-held and cherished
aspirations,
willing now to risk
a different process
to see their dreams
fulfilled.
And all because
God saw the affliction
of His people,
heard the prayers
of faithful little ones

and spoke His Word
and somehow,
somewhere
along the way,
trust crept in.

Christmas came early this year.
Its message, ever old
and ever new
Emmanuel – God is with us.
And God still speaks His Word,
that we, who have received
so great a gift
now must set our faces
to walk with resolution
the road to His shalom.
That together we will build
the peace,
together we will stand
against the monsters
of sectarianism and division,
enraged now
as they see slip
from their grasp
the spoils of war.
Together we will speak
and live the Word
of forgiveness,
of acceptance of difference,
of unity in diversity,
of mutual hospitality,

and room enough for all.
This is our pledge
and this we can do,
because somehow,
somewhere,
along the way
trust crept in.

Trust,
of its very nature
so fragile,
so hard to come by,
so easily lost,
precious commodity,
gift of God
to be treasured and nurtured.
Trust
that calls us to believe
a Light now shines
in Ireland
that no darkness
will ever be able
to extinguish,
because somehow,
somewhere,
along the way
God crept in
– in Jesus –
and Christmas came early.